A Midsummer Night's Dream

Recent Titles in
Greenwood Guides to Shakespeare

Henry V: A Guide to the Play
Joan Lord Hall

Macbeth: A Guide to the Play
H. R. Coursen

Hamlet: A Guide to the Play
W. Thomas MacCary

Julius Caesar: A Guide to the Play
Jo McMurtry

Romeo and Juliet: A Guide to the Play
Jay L. Halio

Othello: A Guide to the Play
Joan Lord Hall

The Tempest: A Guide to the Play
H. R. Coursen

King Lear: A Guide to the Play
Jay L. Halio

Love's Labour's Lost: A Guide to the Play
John S. Pendergast

Antony and Cleopatra: A Guide to the Play
Joan Lord Hall

As You Like It: A Guide to the Play
Steven J. Lynch

The Merchant of Venice: A Guide to the Play
Vicki K. Janik

A MIDSUMMER NIGHT'S DREAM

A Guide to the Play

JAY L. HALIO

Greenwood Guides to Shakespeare

Greenwood Press
Westport, Connecticut • London

Library of Congress Cataloging-in-Publication Data

Halio, Jay L.
A midsummer night's dream : a guide to the play / Jay L. Halio.
p. cm.—(Greenwood guides to Shakespeare)
Includes bibliographical references and index.
ISBN 0–313–32190–6 (alk. paper)
1. Shakespeare, William, 1564–1616. Midsummer night's dream. I. Title. II. Series.
PR2827.H294 2003
822.3'3—dc21   2003044070

British Library Cataloguing in Publication Data is available.

Library of Congress Catalog Card Number: 2003044070
ISBN: 0–313–32190–6

First published in 2003

Greenwood Press, 88 Post Road West, Westport, CT 06881
An imprint of Greenwood Publishing Group, Inc.
www.greenwood.com

Printed in the United States of America

The paper used in this book complies with the
Permanent Paper Standard issued by the National
Information Standards Organization (Z39.48–1984).

10 9 8 7 6 5 4 3 2 1

For Diane

CONTENTS

Statue of Puck. By permission of the Folger Shakespeare Library.

PREFACE

Nothing by Shakespeare before *A Midsummer Night's Dream* is its
equal, and in some respects nothing afterward by him surpasses it.
It is his first undoubted masterwork, without flaw, and one of his
dozen or so plays of over-whelming originality and power.

—Harold Bloom

By common consent, *A Midsummer Night's Dream* is one of the happiest
of Shakespeare's comedies and his first unequivocal triumph in that
genre. A perennial favorite in stage performance, it has also been made
into successful films. Students of all ages love to act in the play, especially the play-within-the-play, Peter Quince's "Pyramus and Thisbe,"
which invariably evokes much laughter from audiences both young and
old.

Clearly, a number of things contribute to the popularity of this comedy. In the first place, it is filled with delightful poetry. Shakespeare
composed *A Midsummer Night's Dream* during his so-called lyric period,
which includes *Romeo and Juliet* and *Richard II* as well as the last act
of *The Merchant of Venice*. Oberon's speech at 2.1.249 ff., which begins
"I know a bank where the wild thyme blows," is unrivaled for its beautiful imagery and the mellifluous flow of the verse—notwithstanding the
fact that it introduces the Fairy King's hideous plot against his queen,
Titania. The complexity of the poetry is part of the overall complexity
of the drama, which Shakespeare constructs using several intersecting
planes, or levels, of reality: the fairy world, the court of Theseus and his
aristocracy, the young lovers, and the "rude mechanicals," or humble

workmen, who are based on Shakespeare's knowledge of his own War-wickshire countrymen. If we include the legendary world of Pyramus and Thisbe, then we must add yet another dimension to the play.

The *Dream*'s plot is accordingly also complex, but neither audiences nor readers have any difficulty following its various strands as they proceed from Theseus's court to the magical forest outside Athens and back again to the court. Many wondrous events occur in the forest, which is ruled over by Oberon and his mischievous henchman, Puck, or Robin Goodfellow, as he was also called. Shakespeare drew upon fairy lore for some aspects of this environment, but, as elsewhere, he transformed traditional notions to suit his own purposes. Above all, he seems to be interested in the vagaries of love's passion, which can and does lead young people into what for them are agonizing problems but, seen objectively, provoke a good deal of humor in onlookers.

A Midsummer Night's Dream can, of course, be played for the fun it evokes, and it should be. But fun is not the sum and substance of the play, which upon closer investigation reveals depths upon depths. Shakespeare presents more than one attitude toward love, for example, and it is important to see here, as also in his later comedies, how the different attitudes compare and contrast with each other. Sensory perception, as always, is problematic, and the eyes are especially apt to betray the intellect. Parental control is another important theme in the *Dream*, and modern audiences may experience difficulties in coming to grips with older notions of how much power a parent, especially a father, may wield over his offspring. Similarly, Shakespeare raises questions regarding the relationships of husband and wife: who is the boss, and how should he—for it was always the man in Shakespeare's time—rule over his house-hold?

From another standpoint, *A Midsummer Night's Dream* is also very much about the function of the imagination and the art of performance. One of the most delightful things about Shakespeare's art is that it seldom takes itself too seriously, serious though its purpose and achievement may be. For this reason, Shakespeare gives Theseus his speech about the lover, the madman, and the poet at the beginning of the scene (5.1) in which the play-within-the-play will be performed. During the performance, moreover, he makes several important comments about the nature of stage representation.

By the time he came to write his *Dream*, Shakespeare was approaching the peak of his powers as a dramatic poet and understood well not only the art of playwriting and production, but also the audience's attitudes toward both. At the end of *A Midsummer Night's Dream*, therefore, Puck appeals to the audience to be generous in their response. If the actors, whom he calls "shadows," have displeased them, he begs forgiveness and suggests they consider that the play, whose title after all refers to a dream, should be regarded as nothing more than that. But of course it is a great deal more than that, just as the "insubstantial pageant" that Prospero's masque, his engagement present to his daughter and her fiancé, is more.

This book, then, is designed to help readers plumb some of the depths of *A Midsummer Night's Dream* without becoming too solemn about it all. On the other hand, it covers the major aspects for the serious study of Shakespeare's plays. Hence, the first chapter properly begins with the nature of the text upon which all modern editions are based. Fortunately, the early editions are all quite good, and very few variants appear to distinguish the first edition, the quarto of 1600 (Q1), from the Folio of 1623, the first collected edition of Shakespeare's plays. One important aspect of the texts is the evidence they present of Shakespeare as a reviser for, as John Dover Wilson has pointed out in the New Shakespeare edition (1924), in Theseus's speech about the imagination Shakespeare evidently had further thoughts about what should be included.[1] Because the printer had difficulty with the manuscript at hand, the verse was not correctly aligned; the irregularities thus give us clues about Shakespeare's second thoughts.

The second chapter treats Shakespeare's sources for *A Midsummer Night's Dream* and the contexts in which the play was written. For a long time scholars believed that, given its plot, the play was originally written to help celebrate the wedding of some noble couple. Although several possible wedding festivities have been proposed, none can be proved conclusively to have been the occasion for Shakespeare's composition. Possibly the play was performed at court or at some nobleman's house when Queen Elizabeth was a guest, because there is at least one fairly direct compliment to her; but again, this does not mean that the play was not written for public performance at one of the bankside playhouses.

Fairy lore is an important element in *A Midsummer Night's Dream*, and scholars have traced Shakespeare's debts to folktales and folklore for the characterization of Puck, for example. At the same time they recognize Shakespeare's innovations in the development of his fairies. Oberon and Titania, as well as Theseus and Hippolyta, come from ancient myth and legend, but here too Shakespeare has given us his own characterizations. For the rude mechanicals—Peter Quince and his fellows—Shakespeare needed only to recall his Warwickshire countrymen, although for the story of Pyramus and Thisbe he was indebted to his favorite classical poet, Ovid. In most of his plays scholars have been able to discover plot sources, but like the plot of *The Tempest*, that of *A Midsummer Night's Dream* seems to have been Shakespeare's own invention.

The second chapter also deals with the play's social milieu. Attitudes toward women and children were far different in Shakespeare's time than in our own, and modern audiences may have difficulty in accepting some of them. Women had few rights and children none; husband and father ruled more or less absolutely. This situation precipitates the major actions of *A Midsummer Night's Dream*, which involve both the young lovers and the king and queen of the fairies.

Chapter 3 analyzes the dramatic structure of *A Midsummer Night's Dream*. Shakespeare's play is deeply complex but never confusing. The events of the forest are framed by the setting in Athens, both providing levels, or planes, of reality that Shakespeare explores carefully and confidently. Language is but one means by which the various levels are differentiated, and its uses reward close investigation. Remembering that the scene was the basic building block for Elizabethan drama, readers like directors and producers need to examine how the collocation of scenes helps to develop the overall dramatic structure.

The next chapter considers the major themes in the play. As usual in Shakespearean drama, these are several and varied. Attitudes toward love may be the dominant theme, but it is by no means the only one. The art of performance is another subject that Shakespeare develops, comically but nonetheless seriously, in the scenes where Quince & Co. rehearse and finally present their little play, "Pyramus and Thisbe." Friendship, not only among the workmen, but also between Hermia and Helena, for example, is yet another theme in this play, though it may be subservient to the more important theme of the relation of reality to illusion that the fairies help us examine. Finally, the means by which discord yields to harmony brings the play to its conclusion.

Critics have approached *A Midsummer Night's Dream*, as they have Shakespeare's other plays, from a number of different routes. The fifth chapter considers in detail the ways in which these approaches may provide fruitful and illuminating analyses of this play. These critical approaches are not mutually exclusive but usually complementary to each other. Feminist, or gender, criticism, for example, works closely with psychoanalytical criticism and is in some ways closely indebted to it.

Similarly, the New Historicism and Cultural Materialism are related to each other, though they tend to diverge in certain important respects. The definitions and a sampling of these and other critical approaches, including myth and archetypal criticism, appear in this chapter.

The sixth chapter concentrates upon the play in performance. We need always to remind ourselves that regardless of how beautiful Shakespeare's plays are to read and how fascinating they are to study, they were initially designed to be performed live on stage. Shakespeare was not only a great dramatic poet, he was also—first and foremost—a man of the theater. It was from box office receipts that he, as one of the principal shareholders of his company, became a rich man, enabling him to buy valuable property in Stratford-upon-Avon and make other significant investments. Because of the great diversity and complexity of his plays, and specifically *A Midsummer Night's Dream*, actors and directors have found a myriad of ways to present what Shakespeare wrote. This chapter briefly traces what we suppose the earliest performances must have been like through the changes that occurred after the Restoration of the monarchy in England in 1660 on into the eighteenth century. The nineteenth century then became known for its more grandiose productions as well as the introduction of Felix Mendelssohn's famous overture and incidental music.

The rise of technology has enabled various experimental stages and settings to be tried. In the twentieth century, film and later television became interested in producing versions of Shakespeare's plays, and a number of them succeeded very well in bringing Shakespeare's work to mass audiences via a medium that the author of the plays probably never envisioned (see chapter 7). The relation of stage and film productions is an important one, and students need to discern what they are before attempting to compare and contrast them. The study of the text, or script, is vital in ascertaining the director's approach to production, as are the setting and costume designs, all of which are considered here.

No book can hope to encompass all that has been done or written for any Shakespeare play; hence, an annotated bibliography concludes this guide to *A Midsummer Night's Dream*. It is a selected bibliography perforce; far more extensive bibliographies are available elsewhere. The notes to each chapter will also help direct readers who wish to pursue further certain aspects of the play.

Like every Shakespearean who dares to write about his subject, I owe a great many debts to those who have preceded me. I trust that the notes and bibliography will sufficiently acknowledge the major debts incurred.

For chapter 6 I have drawn heavily—I hope not too heavily—upon my book on *A Midsummer Night's Dream* in the Manchester University Press series, *Shakespeare in Performance*, which has recently appeared in a second, enlarged edition, although my references are to the first one (1994). I am grateful to George Butler, who once again assigned this project to me; to copyeditor Lynn Wheeler; and to my wife, Diane S. Isaacs, who read through the typescript and made numerous suggestions and corrections. To her this book is lovingly dedicated.

NOTE

1. Arthur Quiller-Couch and John Dover Wilson, eds., *A Midsummer Night's Dream*. Cambridge, England: Cambridge University Press, 1924.

1

TEXTUAL HISTORY

Although written in 1595–96 (see chapter 2), *A Midsummer Night's Dream* was not published until 1600. The entry for the play, which appears in the Stationers' Register on October 8, 1600, indicates that Thomas Fisher paid sixpence for the entry:

> Tho. ffyssher / Entred for his copie vnder the handes of Mr Rodes / and the Wardens. A booke called / A mydsomer nightes dreame. vj^d

How Fisher came into possession of the manuscript for publication is not known, but most scholars agree that since it was properly entered in the Register and the publication displays a reasonably good text, the quarto (Q1) may have been authorized by Shakespeare's company.[1] This was the first play Fisher, a draper turned bookseller, published, since he only became a member of the Stationers' Company that year.[2] He was not long in the trade, and his association with Shakespeare's acting company may have been limited to this one publication.[3]

EARLY EDITIONS

The 1600 quarto was printed by Richard Bradock, who published a number of plays in quarto between 1598 and 1602.[4] The title page of this quarto reads as follows:

A
Midsommer nights
dreame.
As it hath beene sundry times pub-
lickely acted, by the Right honoura-
ble, the Lord Chamberlaine his
seruants.
Written by William Shakespeare.
[Printer's device]
Imprinted at London, for *Thomas Fisher*, and are to be soulde at his shoppe,
at the Signe of the White Hart, in *Fleetestreete*. 1600.[5]

This quarto, signed 1–4, collates A–H[4]. The text begins on A2[r] and ends on H4[v]. Most pages contain thirty-five lines of text, except for D2[v] and the first four pages of sheet G. These pages contain thirty-five lines of text, except for G2[r], which contains only thirty-two lines.[6] These differences are of significance only when considering the reprinting of Q1 in the second quarto (1619), on which the First Folio (1623) was based.

Evidence from running titles and recurring type indicate that one compositor rather than two set Q1 by formes, but certain irregularities suggest that the compositor might have set the text seriatim between one or two pages in certain sheets, as in the first four pages of sheet G.[7] The eight extant copies of Q1 have been collated and reveal only five press variants in four of the sixteen formes: the inner and outer formes of Sheet E, and the inner formes of sheets A and F. The inner forme of sheet A exists in three states.[8] The variants involve merely typos; for example, a turned letter or a mistaken "ro" for "to" on sheet A.[9] More substantive corrections, such as the mislineation of Theseus's speech at the beginning of act 5, are not evident, a matter that suggests proof correction was neither thorough nor systematic. This was, after all, only a play and not more serious material, such as sermons or historical tracts. On the other hand, because so few copies of Q1 remain extant (and therefore collation is so limited), it is difficult to determine just how carefully proof correction was in fact done.

Scholars agree that the copy for Q1 must have been Shakespeare's so-called foul papers, that is, his early draft of the play. (The fair copy, made into a promptbook with the Master of Revels seal of approval, would be retailed by the acting company.) Indications of foul-papers provenance are the spellings deemed peculiar to Shakespeare, such as his predilection for double "o" (as in "mooue" and "proove") and the use of "maruailes" for "marvelous." Stage directions, or the absence of them, also suggest authorial provenance. For example, often they tend to be rather more vague than specific, as at 3.1, *"Enter the Clownes,"* and at 4.2.0, *"Enter* Quince, Flute, Thisby *and the rabble."* The latter example is especially interesting as it gives both Flute's name and that of his role in the play-within-the-play but does not give the names of the other members of Quince's troupe. Elsewhere, there is a tendency to vary speech headings, as for example in 2.1, where some headings use "Puck" and others "Rob [in] [Goodfellow]."[10]

Of special interest are the signs of revision that occur in Q1, as revealed particularly in the lineation of 5.1.2–27. John Dover Wilson long ago analyzed the passage and demonstrated what apparently had happened to cause the mislineation here and later in the scene.[11] In his view, which has since been universally accepted, Shakespeare inserted, probably in the margin, some additional lines into the passage he originally wrote in regular iambic pentameters. The compositor did his best to incorporate the additional lines in Theseus's speech, but in so doing he seriously disturbed the meter. I reprint the passage below as it appears in Q1, italicizing the added lines and inserting a slant line, /, to show the proper lineation, as it appears in modern edited texts. (Italicized proper names appear as such in Q1.)

Hip. Tis strange, my *Theseus,* that these louers speake of.

The. More straunge then true. I neuer may beleeue
These antique fables, nor these Fairy toyes.
Louers, and mad men haue such seething braines,
Such shaping phantasies, that apprehend / more,
Then coole reason euer comprehends. / The lunatick,
The louer, and the Poet / are of imagination all compact. /
One sees more diuels, then vast hell can holde:
That is the mad man. The louer, all as frantick,
Sees *Helens* beauty in a brow of *Aegypt.*
The Poets eye, in a fine frenzy, rolling, / doth glance
From heauen to earth, from earth to heauen. / And as
Imagination bodies forth / the formes of things
Vnknowne: the Poets penne / turnes them to shapes,
And giues to ayery nothing, / a locall habitation,
And a name. / Such trickes hath strong imagination,
That if it would but apprehend some ioy,
It comprehends some bringer of that ioy.
Or in the night, imagining some feare,
How easie is a bush suppos'd a Beare?

The following lines in act 5 (up to line 84) show similar discrepancies, which Wilson accounted for in the same way.[12]

A second quarto (Q2), falsely dated 1600 and purportedly printed by James Roberts, appeared in 1619. It was in fact printed in William Jaggard's shop as one of the series of quartos that his friend Thomas Pavier attempted to pass off as the originals. Pavier had the idea of producing a collection of Shakespeare's plays before Shakespeare's colleagues, Heminges and Condell, gathered his works for the First Folio several years later. Stymied in his attempt to produce the collection, Pavier resorted to these deceptions to recover some of the costs already expended on the scheme.

Q2 is essentially a page-for-page reprint of Q1, except for the first four pages of sheet G, where the standard thirty-five lines of text appear instead of Q1's thirty-four. The additional type space allowed the compositor to correct some of the mislineation in 5.1, but Q2 has no real authority. Like other reprints, it corrects some errors but introduces others.[13] It is important only because a marked-up copy of this quarto was apparently used as copy for the play that Jaggard's compositors used in setting the text in the Folio of 1623.

The Folio, set from the Q2 reprint,[14] nevertheless has several significant alterations of copy. These may derive from some playhouse manuscript, since it adds or clarifies a goodly number of stage directions.[15] At the same time, it further corrupts the text beyond the errors introduced by Q2—a characteristic of many reprints. Among the most notable alterations is the substitution of Egeus for Philostrate in act 5. Harold Brooks and R. A. Foakes speculate that the change was introduced to eliminate one speaking part, insofar as Philostrate has no lines in his only other appearance in act 1.[16] Furthermore, Lysander reads the list of entertainments presented to Theseus, who comments upon them in F, as opposed to the Q1 version, in which Theseus both reads and comments. Presumably the change was to make the presentation more dramatic and to involve in dialogue at least one of the young lovers who otherwise remain silent throughout this part of the scene.[17] Another change is the stage direction at 5.1.125, where the entrance of Pyramus and Thisbe is preceded by "*Tawyer with a Trumpet before him.*" William Tawyer, a member of the King's Men, died in 1625; he was a servant to John Heminges, a shareholder along with Shakespeare in the company. The inclusion of this stage direction clearly points to a promptbook source and, by extension, the source for other alterations, which may have been introduced after the King's Men began using the Blackfriars Theatre in 1609.[18]

One of the more problematical stage directions appears at the end of act 3: *"They sleepe all the Act."* Act divisions were introduced later than the original composition of *A Midsummer Night's Dream* (Q1 and Q2 have none), and they appear somewhat arbitrarily in Folio.[19] Although a five-act structure may have been in Shakespeare's mind from the start,[20] the dramatist obviously conceived of the play as a continuous action. This is what the Q stage directions, which omit *"They sleepe all the Act,"* indicate. Whatever the case, it is also clear that the couples at the end of 3.2 do remain on stage, as none of the texts provides an exit for them. Some editors speculate on the meaning of "Act" as referring not to the usual modern sense, but to the interval between the acts. Another possible meaning of "Act" is the music played during the interval. Foakes, however, argues convincingly that the probable meaning in this context is that the lovers remain on stage asleep all during the next act until awakened by Theseus's huntsman (4.2.135). This interpretation is reinforced by the Folio stage direction at 4.1.98, *"Sleepers Lye still,"* indicating that the couples remain asleep all this while.[21]

The Folio of 1623 was reprinted in 1632, 1663–64, and 1685. Like other reprints, they have no textual authority, despite their attempts to correct some obvious errors, which subsequent editions have accepted.

EIGHTEENTH-CENTURY EDITIONS

Modern editing of Shakespeare's plays may be said to begin with Nicholas Rowe's edition of 1709. Rowe corrected some of the mislineation in act 5 and more in his third edition of 1714; Lewis Theobald corrected still more in 1733.[22] Further corrections involving stage directions were also introduced, particularly necessary entrances and exits and clarifying directions. While eighteenth-century editors are notorious for their attempts to improve on Shakespeare's versification and diction, sometimes rewriting whole passages, *A Midsummer Night's Dream* seems to have escaped such interventions, at least on a wholesale scale. On the other hand, the editors not only divided the plays into numbered scenes according to the neoclassical conventions they observed, they also introduced scene locations, a practice abandoned only as recently as the late twentieth century. For example, in Alexander Pope's edition of 1723, the designation *"Act II. Scene I."* is followed by *"The Wood."*, after which the entrance of the characters appears: "*Enter a Fairy at one door, and* Puck *or* Robin-goodfellow *at another.*" This entrance replicates Q1, except that Puck is referred to by both of his names. Pope further departs from Q and F in speech headings and uses "Puck" instead of "Robin" in this scene, following his predecessor Rowe. Again, Pope divides 2.1 into four scenes, marking a new scene when Oberon, Titania, and their trains enter (2.1.59), when Demetrius and Helena enter (2.1.187), and when they depart (2.1.244). As we might expect, the spelling throughout is modernized, and punctuation reflects eighteenth-century practice as well.

Neoclassical decorum also dictated a "purer" form of drama, including comedy, on the stage. Hence, acting editions of *A Midsummer Night's Dream* often split off the low comedy of the rude mechanicals into such "drolls" as *Bottom the Weaver* (1646), a short play that omits the opening scene with Theseus and Hippolyta and all of the lovers' plot, though it retains Oberon's scheme to enchant Titania. This plot enables the comedy of Bottom with the ass's head to proceed and Titania's infatuation with him, ending with the "Pyramus and Thisbe" farce and a dance.[23] Much of Shakespeare's language is retained, but some additional lines are inserted, and two "Lords" instead of Demetrius and Lysander comment on the mechanicals' playlet. In 1716 Richard Leveridge adapted the comic underplot as a "Comic Masque" called *Pyramus and Thisbe.* It combines 1.2 with part of 3.1 essentially as Shakespeare wrote the scenes, except for the exclusion of Bottom's "translation." It then moves directly to the play-within-the-play, adding some new characters (Theseus, Hippolyta, and the others are omitted) and new lines that are sung by Lion and Moonshine. It concludes with an entirely new epilogue, since Puck is no longer one of the dramatis personae.[24]

Although Shakespeare's *Dream* was not popular on the stage in the Augustan period and was seldom produced except in severely curtailed form as afterpieces, scholars continued to edit it along with all of his other works.[25] In the middle of the eighteenth century David Garrick derived an opera from it called *The Fairies.*[26] The opera eliminated the low comedy altogether and interspersed among Shakespeare's lines a considerable number of "airs." The opera concluded not with "Pyramus and Thisbe" but with Theseus's overriding Egeus's will, Helena's air "Love's a tempest," and a chorus of joy, as all the lovers march to Hymen's altar to declare their vows. A few years later, George Colman produced, as an afterpiece, a two-act version called *A Fairy Tale* (1763), designed to capitalize on the expenditures for his adaptation of *A Mid-*

summer Night's Dream, which apparently failed badly after a single performance.[27] *A Fairy Tale* begins like Leveridge's adaptation, but this one
introduces songs much earlier, both in the first scene and in the ones
that follow. Puck is retained along with the comedy of Bottom and his
ass's head. The piece ends, however, not with "Pyramus and Thisbe" but
with Oberon and Titania's reconciliation in 4.1 and "A Dance of Fairies."

MODERN EDITIONS

Recent editions of *A Midsummer Night's Dream* tend to retain act and
scene divisions, though not those adopted by the neoclassically oriented
eighteenth-century editors, and the tendency is to make them appear
much less intrusive. The Penguin edition, for example, places the des-
ignations in the margin, not above the text, to convey the impression of
continuous action found in the quartos. The principle followed is that
generally a new scene begins when the stage is entirely cleared and a
new set of characters enter. (An exception in *Dream* is the end of act 3,
as noted above.) Spelling and punctuation continue to reflect contemporary practice, which is a surprising fact, given that editions of the
works of other Renaissance authors, such as Edmund Spenser and John
Milton, retain the original orthography. Old-spelling editions of Shakespeare are rare, and none are available in inexpensive popular editions
or school texts.

A Midsummer Night's Dream is of course included in all editions of
Shakespeare's complete works. In almost every one of these editions,
the play begins with a critical introduction, usually covering sources and
textual matters, but mainly concentrating on interpretations of dramatic
structure, themes, and characters—all this besides the general introductions that include sections on Shakespeare's life and times, his development as an artist, London theaters and dramatic companies, other
editions of Shakespeare, as well as a survey of criticism and an extensive
though selective bibliography. A substantial number of footnotes on each
page of text supplies a running critical commentary and glossary.

A good example of editions that include the complete works is the
Riverside Shakespeare, edited by G. Blakemore Evans, now with the
assistance of J. J. Tobin in its second edition (1997). It includes an introduction to *A Midsummer Night's Dream* by Anne Barton. Another
good example of this kind of edition is David Bevington's *Complete
Works of Shakespeare* (4th ed., 1997), which, like the Riverside, arranges
the plays chronologically by genre but, unlike the Riverside, uses Be-

vington's own introductions to each play. *The Arden Shakespeare* contains the complete works, each one edited by a different scholar. It is actually a compendium of Arden 2 editions, with a few of the more recent editions in the Arden 3 series, supervised by general editors Richard Proudfoot, Ann Thompson, and David Scott Kastan, but, like the Oxford *Complete Works* (see below), it excludes commentary notes. *A Midsummer Night's Dream* in this collection is from Arden 2 by Harold Brooks (see below). *The Complete Pelican Shakespeare* (1969; general editor Alfred Harbage) likewise has texts edited by divers hands. The *Dream* here is edited by Madeleine Doran. The Pelican Shakespeare is also being newly edited under the general editorship of A. R. Braunmuller and Stephen Orgel.

The Oxford's *William Shakespeare: The Complete Works*, edited by Stanley Wells and Gary Taylor (1986), unlike most of the complete works mentioned above, has very brief introductions and no commentary notes, although it does include a glossary at the back.[28] It also differs from the other complete works in arranging the works solely by chronological order, not by genre. The compact edition is available in both hardback and paperback versions and is among the least expensive of the complete works. In the text of *Dream*, as in the texts of other plays, the Oxford editors introduce a number of innovations. For example, 3.2 is divided into two scenes, with a new scene indicated after Demetrius's exit with Puck at 3.2.412 and before Lysander's entrance. The Norton complete works, under Stephen Greenblatt's general supervision, adopts the Oxford texts but adds commentary notes and more extensive introductions by various critics. Greenblatt is the author also of the introduction to the *Dream*, in which he discounts completely the notion that the play was written for a wedding or even performed at one.

Many excellent single editions of *A Midsummer Night's Dream* also exist, the most useful of which are described next. One of the best is the volume edited by R. A. Foakes in the New Cambridge Shakespeare (1979). Its concise introduction (41 pages) covers the date and occasion of the play, its sources and stage history, and a critical interpretation ("The play in the mind"); a textual analysis follows the text. Its useful collation of variant readings and accepted or proposed emendations appears in smaller type beneath the text of the play and above the critical commentary. An appendix consists of a further note on sources followed by a reading list of important books and articles. The volume in the Oxford series, edited by Peter Holland (1994), arranges its extensive introduction quite differently, mainly under the rubrics of the characters' names, but it includes a good deal of the stage history and other matters. Like the New Cambridge edition, its collation appears beneath the text and before the commentary notes. Its single appendix is devoted to "Shakespeare's Revisions of Act 5." Unlike the Cambridge series, each volume in the Oxford series includes a useful index of words glossed in the commentary, a selective group of authors, and productions referred to in the introduction, commentary, and appendices.

Harold Brooks edited *A Midsummer Night's Dream* for Arden 2 (1979). Its extensive, 163-page introduction covers many aspects of the play, and several appendices include excerpts from sources and lengthy discussions of four textual cruxes. The page of text follows the same format as the New Cambridge and Oxford editions, but it is, if anything, fuller. These three editions are all available in both hardback form and much less expensive paperbacks. The new Pelican edition, edited by Russ McDonald (2000), contains a good introduction, notes at the bottom of each page but no collation (adopted variant readings appear at the end of the note on the text, pp. lii–liii). The Folger Library edition, edited by Barbara Mowat and Paul Werstein (1993), adopts a completely different format, one that many readers like. The text of the play appears on the right-hand pages; notes and illustrations appear on the facing pages. A lengthy introduction focuses on the interpretation of the play, Shakespeare's life, his theater, the publication of his plays, and the text. At the end of the volume, after the textual notes, are a critical essay by Catherine Belsey, a reading list, and a key to famous lines and phrases. John F. Andrews's Everyman edition follows the same facing-page format; it has an introduction by the editor and an essay by F. Murray Abraham on the play in performance. This edition, like others in the Everyman series, while using modern spelling preserves significant older spellings and punctuation where puns and other aspects of Shakespeare's language, in the opinion of the editor, need to be preserved.

The Signet edition by Wolfgang Clemen, originally published in 1963, has an updated bibliography and an introduction by the general editor, Sylvan Barnet. A number of excerpts from critical studies by William Hazlitt, John Russell Brown, Linda Bamber, and others appear at the end of the volume, along with an essay written by Barnet on the play on stage and screen (1986; 1998). The Bantam edition, taken from David Bevington's complete works, incorporates three other comedies: *The Taming of the Shrew*, *The Merchant of Venice*, and *Twelfth Night*. Bevington's text appears also in the Bedford series, "Texts and Contexts," with a large selection of historical documents from Queen Elizabeth I's speech to Parliament on marriage and succession (1566) to Sir Thomas North's translation of Plutarch's "Life of Theseus" (1579) and John Stow's *Annals of England* (1601). A good many other editions of the play, including Applause Books' paperback reprint of the Folio text, are also in print in almost every conceivable format and price range, from school texts to extensive scholarly volumes.

NOTES

1. See Harold Brooks, ed., *A Midsummer Night's Dream* (Arden Shakespeare 2). London: Methuen, 1979, xxi.

2. See R. A. Foakes, ed., *A Midsummer Night's Dream* (New Cambridge Shakespeare). Cambridge, England: Cambridge University Press, 1984, 135.

3. Ibid.

4. For a summary of Bradock's career as a printer of plays, and his association with Fisher, see Tom Berger, *A Midsummer Night's Dream, 1600*. The Malone Society Reprints, 1995, 157: viii–ix.

5. Ibid., v. Here and elsewhere where the early editions are quoted, the long "s" has not been preserved, nor have the ligatures; otherwise, the original spelling has been retained.

6. Ibid.

7. Robert K. Turner, "Printing Methods and Textual Problems in *A Midsummer Night's Dream*, Q1," *Studies in Bibliography* 15 (1962), 39.

8. See Berger, vi, for further details on the collation.

9. Ibid., vii–viii.

10. See W. W. Greg, *The Shakespeare First Folio*. Oxford: Clarendon Press, 1955, 240–42; and Foakes, *Midsummer Night's Dream*, 135–36; Brooks, *Midsummer Night's Dream*, xxii–xxiv; Malone Society Reprint, ix. Although some extant period promptbooks also reveal similar inconsistencies, the preponderance of them here as well as their kinds have convinced editors that foul-papers were in fact used as copy for Q1.

11. See Arthur Quiller-Couch and John Dover Wilson, eds., *A Midsummer Night's Dream* (The New Shakespeare). Cambridge, England: Cambridge University Press, 1924, 80–86. Wilson further argued that Shakespeare revised the play during several different time periods. According to Wilson, the original text goes much farther back to about 1592 and was later revised from time to time to the form in which it appears in Q1 (see 94–97). His view has not been generally accepted. (See, e.g., Greg, *First Folio*, 242–43; Foakes, *Midsummer Night's Dream*, 137–38.) On Shakespeare as a reviser, see Grace Ioppolo, *Revising Shakespeare*. Cambridge, Mass.: Harvard University Press, 1991.

12. See also Janis Lull, "Textual Theory, Literary Interpretation, and the Last

Act of *A Midsummer Night's Dream*," in *"A Midsummer Night's Dream": Critical Essays*, ed. Dorothea Kehler, 241–58. New York: Garland, 1998. Lull argues persuasively that the additions and alterations in Theseus's speeches in this act (even beyond line 83) serve to develop his character further; he evolves "from rationalist to imaginationist." "Under his new wife's subtle but persistent influence," Lull points out, "Theseus becomes conscious first of the pressing importance of the irrational in his private life, then of some of the public uses of imagination in an Athenian community grounded on courtesy and reason" (p. 245). Recent stage productions also tend to take this view (see chapter 6 of this volume).

13. Foakes, *Midsummer Night's Dream*, 138.

14. The typesetting of F has been analyzed in detail by Charlton Hinman, *The Printing and Proof Reading of the First Folio of Shakespeare*. Oxford: Clarendon Press, 1963, 2: 415–26.

15. Greg, *First Folio*, 246; Brooks, *Midsummer Night's Dream*, xxviii–xxxii; Foakes, *Midsummer Night's Dream*, 139.

16. Brooks, *Midsummer Night's Dream*, xxxii; Foakes, *Midsummer Night's Dream*, 141.

17. Foakes, *Midsummer Night's Dream*, 141.

18. Brooks, *Midsummer Night's Dream*, xxx; Foakes, *Midsummer Night's Dream*, 140–41.

19. See Gary Taylor, "The Structure of Performance: Act-Intervals in the London Theatres, 1576–1642," in *Shakespeare Reshaped, 1606–1623*, ed. Gary Taylor and John Jowett, 3–50. Oxford: Clarendon Press, 1993. After 1616, and probably earlier, plays were divided into five acts, with intervals between the acts (p. 4).

20. See G. K. Hunter, "Were There Act Pauses on Shakespeare's Stage," *Renaissance Drama* (1976), 18, 27; cited by Foakes, *Midsummer Night's Dream*, 142, who questions this point, noting that Philip Henslowe sometimes paid playwrights for contributing one or more acts to a play. Compare Taylor, "Structure of Performance," 3.

21. Foakes, *Midsummer Night's Dream*, 143.

22. Lull, "Textual Theory," 242–43.

23. See the reprint of this droll, edited by J. O. Halliwell, privately printed for him in London, 1860.

24. A different adaptation, called "A Mock Opera" and dated 1765, was performed at Covent Garden. It eliminated all but the play-within-the-play, which it turned into an operetta.

25. For a list of editions, see D. Allen Carroll and Gary Jay Williams, eds., *A Midsummer Night's Dream: An Annotated Bibliography*. New York: Garland, 1986.

26. The opera dates from 1755. My analysis is based upon the 1765 London edition as performed at the Theatre Royal in Drury Lane. It includes songs from

Shakespeare, Milton, Waller, Dryden, and others, with music composed by "Mr. Smith," as proclaimed by the title page.

27. My analysis of *A Fairy Tale* is based on the 1763 London edition printed for J. and R. Tonson. For further information on these adaptations, see George Winchester Stone, "*A Midsummer Night's Dream* in the Hands of Garrick and Colman," *PMLA* 54 (1939), 467–82.

28. A textual analysis of the play for this edition, containing other material as well as a collation, appears in Stanley Wells and Gary Taylor, with John Jowett and William Montgomery, *William Shakespeare: A Textual Companion*. Oxford: Clarendon Press, 1987, 279–87.

2

CONTEXTS AND SOURCES

The original occasion for the composition of *A Midsummer Night's Dream* has been much disputed. Was it written for the wedding of some grand personages? A number of such weddings have been suggested, but none has been conclusively proved to be the occasion for the first performance. To judge by stylistic evidence and other indications, however, we can be reasonably certain that the play was written in the mid-1590s. This would place the play, rightly, among Shakespeare's so-called lyric plays, which include *Richard II* and *Romeo and Juliet*. Titania's reference to foul weather and the seasons' inversion (2.1.82–114), furthermore, may reflect the bad summers of 1595 and 1596.[1] The play could not have been written later than 1598, since it is one of the plays Francis Meres mentions in his *Palladis Tamia*, registered for publication in that year.

A PLAY ORIGINALLY FOR PRIVATE PERFORMANCE?

Since the play is one of the shortest in the canon, running to only 2,136 lines (compared to over 3,000 for *Romeo and Juliet* and almost 4,000 for *Hamlet*), some scholars believe it must have been written primarily for private rather than public performance; the content of the play also points to a ceremonial event, namely a marriage feast.[2] Accordingly, several such events have been proposed. E. K. Chambers lists six late-sixteenth-century weddings that scholars have advanced as possibilities, beginning with the wedding of Robert Earl of Essex and Frances Lady

Sidney in April or May 1590 and ending with Henry Lord Herbert and Anne Russell's wedding at Blackfriars on June 16, 1600.[3] The first is of course too early, unless one accepts the conjecture that the play reveals several layers of composition, going back to that earlier period—a theory rejected by most scholars.[4] The later date is possible for a revival of the play, although no hard evidence exists to prove that it was, in fact, performed then. Since the play pays compliments to Queen Elizabeth (see, for example, Oberon's description of the "fair vestal throned in the west," 2.1.148–64), some have thought that she was present at that performance, but again, no conclusive evidence has been brought forward to prove that she was.

Of course, the queen might have been present at other similar occasions. Two such occasions fall within the realm of possibility, that is, the accepted time frame for the composition of the play: the wedding of William Stanley, Earl of Derby, and Elizabeth Vere at Greenwich on January 26, 1595; and that of Thomas Berkeley and Elizabeth Carey at Blackfriars on February 19, 1596. Chambers remained unconvinced that the *Dream* was actually performed at the Stanley-Vere wedding and tended to favor the occasion of the Berkeley-Carey ceremony.[5] Elizabeth Carey was one of the queen's goddaughters and the granddaughter of her first cousin and Lord Chamberlain, Henry Lord Hunsdon. Shakespeare's company, the Lord Hunsdon's Men, passed under the patronage of Sir George Carey, who in turn became Lord Hunsdon after his father's demise in 1596. Although it is not certain that Queen Elizabeth attended this wedding, it is likely that she did, and it is likely that the Lord Hunsdon's Men could have been asked to perform a play that would be appropriate for the occasion. No evidence exists, however, to support definitively either assumption.

Another, less likely occasion for the play is the marriage of the Earl of Southampton in 1598 to Elizabeth Vernon, cousin and protegée of the Earl of Essex. Southampton was Shakespeare's patron and Essex was a favorite of the queen, at least at that time. The late date is acceptable only if Shakespeare's revision of the play at that time is also acceptable,[6] an argument rejected by most scholars. Still another wedding has been mentioned as a possible occasion for the play; but, as with the Essex-Sidney one, it is too early: the wedding of the Countess of Southampton and Sir Thomas Heneage on May 2, 1594. Like her son's wedding to Elizabeth Vernon, which was clandestine, the countess's to Sir Thomas caused problems, and both bridegrooms found themselves in disfavor with the queen.[7]

Such speculation has sprouted not only because of the content of the play, but also because of its dramatis personae. While Shakespeare's company usually included two or three boys to perform female roles, it did not have enough for the fairies—Moth, Peaseblossom, Mustardseed, and Cobweb—to perform along with the brides, and doubling these roles, according to some views, was not an option. Hence, these scholars have suggested that the children of a noble family might have been recruited to play roles in the *Dream*. As several modern productions have shown, however, the roles of the fairies need not have been performed by children; the fairies and the mechanicals—Flute, Snout, Snug, and Starveling—can be doubled, though how effectively is another matter.[8] Finally, as Stanley Wells has argued, there is no very compelling reason to believe that *A Midsummer Night's Dream* was not originally intended for the public stage.[9]

MARRIAGE IN ELIZABETHAN ENGLAND

A Midsummer Night's Dream opens with discussions of marriage, an institution that was taken quite seriously in Shakespeare's time. Like any other impatient bridegroom, Theseus is eager to solemnize his marriage to Hippolyta, the Amazonian queen (about which more later). No sooner does he send Philostrate to stir up the Athenian youth to merriments—that is, to celebrate the occasion of his wedding—than Egeus enters with his daughter Hermia and her two suitors, Lysander and Demetrius. He is angry at his daughter's disobedience to his wishes; he wants her to marry Demetrius instead of Lysander, whom she loves. Modern audiences will certainly sympathize with Hermia and not with her father, who seems utterly tyrannical; but Shakespeare's audience would very likely have found nothing unusual in Egeus's behavior. A father reigned supreme in that patriarchal society, and his children were his possessions for him to do with as he chose, as indeed Old Capulet in *Romeo and Juliet* did with his daughter Juliet when he demanded that she wed Count Paris.[10] Arranged marriages were commonplace, certainly among the gentry and nobility. Because divorces were difficult, if not impossible, to obtain, marriage was for life. Romantic love, which Shakespeare appears to support in *A Midsummer Night's Dream*, was scarcely an option. A young person required permission of his or her parents to marry, since it was they who had reason and good sense, aided by experience, to guide their offspring. As the Swiss protestant Heinrich Bullinger wrote in *The Christian State of Matrimony* (1541),

Children may [not] marry without the respect, knowledge, or consent of their parents, under whose authority and jurisdiction they be. . . . [L]aws both natural (divine specially) and civil require the parents' consent to the childrens' marriage, in so much as they judge the promise to be of no value which is made without the knowledge of the parents. . . . For inasmuch as the children are not yet come to perfect discretion, they cannot contract marriage which requireth understanding; yea, they can neither counsel nor help themselves. So in this behalf the consent of their parents is not only necessary, but also good and profitable for them.[11]

Bullinger goes on to say, "Disobedience of children also toward their parents and tutors hath ever been reprehended among all nations," and he invokes the scriptural commandment to honor one's father and mother, arguing that it is never more relevant than in the matter of the contracting of wedlock.[12]

Theseus, as ruler of Athens, at first sides with Egeus in upholding the law. To the father's alternatives held out to Hermia—obey or die— Theseus adds a third: Hermia may become a nun, eschewing forever the company of men and therefore the possibility of any marriage. Of course, by the late sixteenth century, monasteries and convents had been abolished in Reformation England, and in any case nuns were unknown as such in classical times, except possibly for vestal virgins, to which Theseus appears to allude (1.1.70–73, 89–90).[13] These three remain Hermia's hard choices.

FAIRY LORE

Although Shakespeare invented the specific kinds of fairies found in *A Midsummer Night's Dream*, the lore of fairies is much older. Geoffrey Chaucer's Wyf of Bath, for example, speaks of the time of King Arthur when

Al was this land fulfild of fayerye.
The elf-queene, with hir joly compaignye,
Daunced ful ofte in many a grene mede.
This was the olde opinion, as I rede;
I speke of manye hundred yeres ago.
For now kan no man se none elves mo.[14]

This, written 200 years before Shakespeare's play, indicates how ancient the belief in fairies was in England and, by extention, elsewhere. If Chaucer's Wyf believes that people could no longer see fairies, or elves, she does not say that they no longer exist, though she may imply as much. Nevertheless, the beliefs in fairies continued right through Shakespeare's time. Shakespeare's early contemporary, Edmund Spenser, named his great epic romance *The Faerie Queene* (1589–96), although most of the characters in that work are quite unlike the kinds of fairies typical of country lore. His fairy queen, moreover, was in many ways representative of Queen Elizabeth I and a tribute to her.[15]

Fairies were of two sorts—benign and malignant—though belief in both was strongly opposed by the Church.[16] The malignant kind were associated with witchcraft; the benign, with helpful deeds, such as sweeping houses, providing clean water and victuals, and leaving money in shoes.[17] Shakespeare was careful to distinguish the nature of his fairies from malign demons, or "Damnèd spirits" (3.2.388–93). Despite Puck's delight in mischief, to the mortals the fairies in this play are benevolent.[18] It was a matter of common belief, moreover, that fairies were "real and actual beings."[19]

But of what size? Depending on the kind of fairy, the size could vary, from human or more than human height (the heroic fairies, the "aristocrats" among fairy people) to the size of a three-year-old child or the size of an ant (the flower fairies).[20] Shakespeare evidently made use of several kinds: Oberon and Titania seem to be of human size; Titania has no trouble fondling Bottom and holding him in her arms. Her fairy train, on the other hand, as their names suggest, seem to be quite tiny.[21] Did they have wings, as they are often represented in stage productions? That is uncertain. K. M. Briggs notes that the mythologist Andrew Lang gives fairies wings, but it is unclear when they first acquired them. She speculates that it may have been when angels became predominantly feminine,[22] but Shakespeare gives no indication that his fairies are winged. Although Puck can put a girdle around the earth in forty minutes (2.1.175–76), his speed appears to be a function of some other supernatural attribute, not wings.

Oberon, the king of the fairies, derives from a character in Lord Berners's translation of the French romance *Huon of Bordeaux* (1533) and perhaps from Robert Greene's history play *James IV* (ca. 1590), where he appears in the introductory dialogue and later brings in a round of fairies.[23] A play recorded in Henslowe's *Diary*, called "huon of burdoche," was performed during the Christmas season, 1593–94, probably at the Rose Theatre by Lord Sussex's men. In this play, as in Shakespeare's, Oberon is an Eastern fairy (see 2.1.68) with power over nature and the ability to enchant others.[24] Shakespeare changed him from the dwarf with a beautiful face and kingly deportment to the human-sized character we see in the *Dream*, the consort of Titania, Queen of the Fairies, who also was human in stature.

Titania, on the other hand, comes from classical sources, from Ovid's *Metamorphoses*, III.173, where she is also referred to as Diana, goddess of the moon and the chase. She is clearly quite different from Mab, the other fairy queen, whom Mercutio describes in *Romeo and Juliet* (1.4.53–95), both in stature and nature.[25] In Arthur Golding's translation of Ovid, the name "Titania" does not appear; hence, Shakespeare probably remembered her from reading Ovid in the original Latin.[26] Some scholars believe that Shakespeare got the idea for his King and Queen of the Fairies from Chaucer's "The Merchant's Tale," in which they are named Pluto and Proserpine and quarrel about love, sex, and husband-wife relations. Like Pluto and Proserpine, Oberon and Titania take sides with their human counterparts in the narrative action, but Shakespeare further complicated their relationship with their quarrel over the Indian prince, adding a fairy train for each, and introducing Puck.[27]

Puck has a much richer history in fairy lore than Oberon and Titania. Variously called Poake, Puckle, and Pug, he appears as a goblin, an elf, a brownie, or a fairy.[28] His name, Puck, seems to derive from a generic name in Old English signifying a mischievous or even malicious spirit, also known as Robin Goodfellow.[29] Indeed, Shakespeare used both names for him and both attributes of mischief making and benevolence (2.1.32–58). Some scholars believe that, although Puck, or Robin Goodfellow, was well known in country lore, Shakespeare must have read about him in Reginald Scot's *The Discoverie of Witchcraft* (1584), which provides information not only about witches, but also about fairies and transformations. Scot denied that fairies could have passions like human beings, but Shakespeare clearly endowed his fairy king and queen with very human emotions and attitudes.[30]

Although Shakespeare's most extended use of fairies appears in *A Midsummer Night's Dream*, allusions to their existence, both as benign and malevolent spirits, are found in many other plays. Mercutio's description of Queen Mab is only one such example; Mistress Quickly impersonates another version of the fairy queen in 5.5 of *The Merry Wives of Windsor*, with children playing the role of her fairy train; and Marcellus in *Hamlet* 1.1.144 refers to their power of bewitchment.[31] John

Lyly in his play *Gallathea* (ca. 1585) inserted a dance of fairies in 2.3 and otherwise may have influenced Shakespeare's composition (see below), but no other writer has had as pervasive an influence on the conception and representation of fairies in literature as Shakespeare.[32]

THESEUS AND HIPPOLYTA

While the central episodes of *A Midsummer Night's Dream* concern the young lovers and the quarrel between Oberon and Titania, Shakespeare framed his play with scenes involving two legendary characters. For Theseus, the King of Athens, he drew upon two principal sources: Plutarch's *Life of Theseus* in his *Parallel Lives of Noble Greeks and Romans*, translated out of the Greek by James Amyot and into English from the French by Sir Thomas North (1579), and Chaucer's "The Knight's Tale." Theseus was famous not only for being a great statesman, but also for his prowess both in love and war. According to Plutarch, he battled the Amazons, who were at war with Athens, and captured Antiopa, also called Hippolyta, the name used by Shakespeare. After many had died in the battle, peace was concluded "by agreement." A cause of the war, Plutarch suggests, may have been Theseus's "injurie" to Queen Antiopa, "refusing her, to marye with Phaedra." Plutarch is skeptical of this account but admits that, after Atiopa's death, who had given birth to their son, Hippolytus, Theseus married Phaedra.[33] This, and the account Oberon alludes to in the play (2.1.75–80), in which Theseus betrayed Ariadne after she helped him escape from the Labyrinth following his victory over the Minotaur, indicates a good deal about the traditional understanding of Theseus's character. By contrast, Shakespeare opens the play with a more sympathetic Theseus, impatient to marry Hippolyta, the woman he has beaten in battle, and promising to wed her in "another key," no longer doing her injuries with his sword (1.1.16–19).

Shakespeare did not make much of either Hippolyta, whose role in the play is quite small, or her Amazonian heritage. Others did. Amazonian communities and customs, real or imagined, represented a sizable threat to patriarchal dominance in Elizabethan and earlier times. According to Paster and Howard, Amazons "usurped masculine martial and administrative functions, lived apart from men but used them for procreation, cherished and educated their daughters and disposed of their sons, and (in an emblematic rejection of both maternity and sexual allure) burned off a breast in the interests of martial efficiency."[34] None of this is directly relevant to Shakespeare's portrayal of Hippolyta, but it may have some relevance to the representation of Titania, at least as she first appears in *A Midsummer Night's Dream*, defying Oberon and living apart from him with her own train of fairies. It is perhaps for this reason that the roles of Hippolyta and Titania are often doubled in modern productions, as are the roles of Theseus and Oberon (see chapter 6).

From "The Knight's Tale," which opens with a brief account of Theseus's prowess in war and his conquest of Hippolyta, Shakespeare evidently got the idea for the contrast between the amicable relationship and wedding of the older couple and the fraught relationship between the two young men and the woman they each desire.[35] Although Chaucer's tale borders on the tragic, Shakespeare evidently saw a rich comic potential in the young men's competition for fair Emelye; moreover, he complicated the situation by adding another woman, Helena, to enhance his comedy of love's confusion. (At the end of his career Chaucer otherwise adapted the story of Palamon and Arcite in *The Two Noble Kinsmen*.) Several of the incidents in "The Knight's Tale" probably led to scenes Shakespeare developed, such as the hunting episode, when Theseus together with Hippolyta comes upon the lovers (4.1.100 ff.). In Chaucer, Theseus and Hippolyta discover the young men fighting "as it were bulles two," a situation that suggests the quarrel between Lysander and Demetrius over Helena in 3.2.[36] Theseus's change of heart after he first pronounces a death sentence upon Palamon and Arcite may also have suggested the decision of Shakespeare's Theseus to overrule Egeus and allow Lysander and Hermia to marry after all. Philostrate's name may derive from Arcite's disguise in Part II of "The Knight's Tale," when he assumes the role of a page to Emelye.[37]

PETER QUINCE & COMPANY

One does not have to look far to find the origins for Shakespeare's "rude mechanicals" in a *A Midsummer Night's Dream*. They come right out of Shakespeare's own Warwickshire environs. What, one may ask, are they doing in a setting of classical Athens? Like the simple shepherds William and Audrey in *As You Like It* or the common soldiers talking among themselves and with the disguised king in *Henry V*, they add another, basic level of reality to the complex reality that makes up the whole play. Put another way, they help bridge the divide between imagined reality and ordinary existence, bringing play world and mundane experience, actors and audience, closer together.

Bottom, of course, is a special case. Not only his transformation into a creature with an ass's head, but also his interaction with the Fairy Queen sets him apart from his fellows. Furthermore, since he is the only one in the play who is fully conscious at the time of what is happening during that interaction, he is set apart from everyone else, the young lovers especially. The idea for his transformation may derive from several possible sources. In the introduction to his edition, Peter Holland emphasizes how Shakespeare "transmutes a variety of 'sources,' turning materials into contexts, structures of association which the play can choose to play with, develop and differ from, in its own pursuit of the meaning of Bottom's translation."[38]

The most obvious source for Bottom's "translation," most scholars agree, is Lucius Apuleius's *The Golden Ass*, translated into English by William Adlington in 1566. In Book III, chapter 17, Apuleius hopes to transform himself into a bird. Fotis, the servant of a witch called Pamphiles, gives him an ointment for the purpose, but instead of becoming a bird, Apuleius turns into an ass—head to tail, hooves and all—though he retains the sense and understanding of a human being. In this shape, which he retains for a period of time, he encounters a number of women who become fascinated with his massive phallus. They show tenderness and affection toward him, however, in ways that suggest Titania's affectionate regard for Bottom in 4.1, as in his encounter with the "noble and rich Matron" of Corinth.[39] Only after a series of adventures, when Apuleius finally eats a rose, the antidote to his transformation, does he resume his normal shape.

Another influence on Shakespeare's imagination may have been the story of King Midas, as told by Thomas Cooper in *Thesaurus Linguae Romanae et Britannicae* (1565).[40] In the contest between Apollo and Pan as to whose music was superior, Midas was the only one among the judges to choose Pan. For this "grosse judgement" Apollo punished Midas by giving him the long ears of an ass, which he was able to hide from everyone except his barber. Still another incident of a man turned into an ass appears in Scot's *Discoverie of Witchcraft* (1584), which Shakespeare may have consulted or remembered for his treatment of Puck, or Robin Goodfellow, and other fairies, as mentioned above. In Book V, chapter 3, Scot relates the story of an Englishman in Cyprus bewitched of a woman from whom he sought to buy some eggs. Transformed into an ass, he served the woman for three years until a wonderful event led to his restoration as a man and the execution of the witch. In Book XIII, chapter 19, Scot also describes certain experiments that may be performed so that a horse's or ass's head can be set upon a man's shoulders, and vice versa.[41] Other sources for men transformed into asses or wearing ass heads include Brant's *Das Narrenschiff* (The Ship of Fools) and the tradition it launched, which culminated, for example, in Erasmus's *Praise of Folly*.[42]

PYRAMUS AND THISBE

The story of Pyramus and Thisbe is one of several Shakespeare borrowed over the years from his favorite classical author, Ovid. It appears in the *Metamorphoses*, Book IV, lines 67–201, as translated by Golding (1567).[43] The two young people were close neighbors and fell in love, but their parents opposed their union. They therefore had to carry on secretly, using signs, until they discovered a cranny in the wall separating their houses that no one else knew about. Through this cranny in the wall they whisper to each other but, addressing the wall, they lament that they still cannot embrace or kiss. Instead, they have to kiss the "parget," or roughcast, on either side of the wall.[44] At length, unable to bear separation any longer, they agree to steal out of their fathers' houses at night and meet under a mulberry tree by a spring at "*Ninus* Tumb" outside of the town.

Unluckily, as Thisbe awaits Pyramus's arrival on this moonlit night, a lioness, surfeited with a slaughtered cow, her lips besmeared with blood, comes to drink at the spring. Frightened, Thisbe runs away to hide, leaving behind her mantle, which the lioness, after drinking her fill, finds and tears to pieces. When Pyramus arrives, he notices a lion's paw and then the bloodied mantle and concludes that he has inadvertently been the cause of his lover's death. Distraught and upbraiding himself, he takes the bloody mantle to the tree, weeping and kissing it, and kills himself with his sword. His blood spurts up "As when a Conduit pipe is crackt," staining the hitherto white mulberries a "deepe darke purple colour." When Thisbe returns, fearing to disappoint her lover, she notices how the berries have turned color and then spies Pyramus "sprawling with his dying limmes." He opens his eyes once upon hearing Thisbe's lament, but he dies without speaking. After making her long complaint, Thisbe joins him in death. Before taking up his sword, she decrees, "Blacke be the colour of thy fruite and mourninglike alway, / Such as the murder of us twaine may evermore bewray."

Shakespeare has his mechanicals follow the outlines of the story, omitting only the details of the mulberry tree's metamorphosis and changing the lioness to a lion. He adds the character of Moonshine, animates Wall, and gives Lion some explanatory lines. Golding's fourteeners may have suggested the old-fashioned poetic style (in rhymed pentameters, not fourteeners, however) that Shakespeare uses for the play-within-the-play.[45] The mechanicals take their production seriously, worrying over issues that are as relevant today as they were then, such as the relation of fiction to reality, audience reaction, and the like. The ways in which they solve what seem to them to be huge problems—as well as their performance overall—may strike us, as it does the stage audience, as very funny. Doubtless Shakespeare intended it to be—for good purpose. But the mechanicals' puzzlement at their audience's reaction is genuine. For this reason and for others, during the rehearsals for his 1970 production of the *Dream*, Peter Brook warned his actors not to overdo the farcical aspects of "Pyramus and Thisbe," as performed by Quince's troupe.[46]

Although Ovid was most likely Shakespeare's principal source, the story of Pyramus and Thisbe was well known. Chaucer included it in *The Legend of Good Women*, and I. Thomson's poem "New Sonet of Pyramus and Thisbe" appeared in Clement Robinson's *Handefull of Pleasant Delites* (1584), which may have given Shakespeare the stanza form for the dying speeches of the lovers.[47] A play in manuscript, "The Tragedy of Pyramus and Thisbe," which may have been written in the sixteenth century, is in the British Library, although Chambers believed it was written a seventeenth-century Cambridge poet, Nathaniel Richards. Archaic in style, it is the sort of thing, Bullough suggests, that Shakespeare was satirizing.[48]

OTHER SOURCES AND ALLUSIONS

Before electing to see "Pyramus and Thisbe" performed, Theseus reads the list Philostrate gives him of other possible entertainments. The first one he rejects is "The battle with the Centaurs, to be sung / By an Athenian eunuch to the harp" (5.1.43–44). The reason Theseus gives for rejecting it is that he has already told Hippolyta the story "In glory of my kinsman, Hercules" (45–46). Theseus himself had fought the Centaurs along with Hercules when they invaded the wedding celebration of Pirithous and Hippodamia,[49] but other reasons may explain the rejection. For example, the account of an intrusion of disorderly creatures at a wedding celebration seems hardly fitting for this wedding celebration, and a eunuch singing it would hardly seem appropriate, either, for the occasion.

"The riot of the tipsy Bacchanals" is the next entertainment Theseus rejects. It refers to the revenge of the Thracian women upon Orpheus, who tore him apart in a Dionysian frenzy for the offense he gave them. Although Bullough thinks this story, which includes an accolade to love and fidelity, might be appropriate for the occasion,[50] a drunken rout ending in death and mutilation does not seem eminently suitable, and, anyway, Theseus dismisses it as "an old device" which he has already seen. Nor does the allegory of "The thrice three Muses mourning for the death / Of learning, late deceased in beggary" (5.1.51–52), which Theseus suspects is "some satire keen and critical, / Not sorting with a nuptial ceremony" (54–55), seem appropriate. Scholars have burned a good deal of oil trying to find the allusion to the specific writer whose death may be alluded to here. Among those nominated for the honor is Shakespeare's contemporary, the playwright Robert Greene, who died in poverty in 1592. Torquato Tasso, the Italian poet laureate, who died in April 1595, is another. But as R. A. Foakes argues in his note to these lines, poets and scholars were proverbially poor, and complaints about the neglect of learning and scholarship were, then as now, commonplace.[51]

DREAM THEORY

From its title to Puck's epilogue, *A Midsummer Night's Dream* refers to the play as a dream, suggesting not only the nature of the events it dramatizes, but also a close relationship between theater and dream, or reality and fantasy. Shakespeare had done this earlier in *The Taming of the Shrew*. Christopher Sly in the Induction is made to believe that what he is experiencing is not a dream or fantasy but reality, though the reverse is of course true. At the end of *The Taming of a Shrew*, which some scholars believe bears a close connection with Shakespeare's play and may, in fact, reflect an earlier version of it, Sly awakens at the end and realizes that he has indeed had a wonderful dream, that he has learned from it, and that he can now return to his shrewish wife with the knowledge of how to tame her.[52] Elsewhere Shakespeare makes other good use of dreams. In *Romeo and Juliet* the eponymous characters refer to dreams they have had, and in *Richard III* dreams are dramatized powerfully on the eve of the battle of Bosworth Field. While a distinction between dream and vision may be made, as Puck does at 5.1.401–6, the concepts are close enough in kind so that Oberon links them synonymously at 3.2.370–71.[53] Nevertheless, Bottom is wise enough to realize that what he has experienced is not a dream but "a most rare vision" (4.1.200).

The interpretation of dreams is at least as old as Genesis where Jacob at Bethel dreams of angels ascending and descending upon a ladder to heaven (Gen. 28), and Joseph interprets several dreams, most importantly Pharoah's dreams of the fat and lean kine (Gen. 41). Classical theory includes works by Plato and Aristotle, but more important for the Renaissance was the *Oneirocritica* of Artemidorus of Daldis.[54] According to Marjorie Garber (6), Artemidorus based his theory on the principle of association, which links his theory to the fundamental principle developed later by Sigmund Freud. But whereas Artemidorus was interested in the associations of the interpreter, Freud was concerned with those of the dreamer—the approach with which we are most familiar today. Artemidorus, moreover, stressed the ambiguity of dream symbols, an aspect of dreams Shakespeare exploits in a number of plays, as in the example of Calphurnia's dream in *Julius Caesar* (2.2.76–90). Puns and word-play—language generally—are thus highly significant in dream interpretation.[55]

Shakespeare, of course, was not the first or only poet to use dreams as a serious element in his work. Among English poets before him, Chaucer is most noteworthy, as indicated by such poems as his *Book of the Duchess, The Legend of Good Women,* and *The Parliament of Fowles,* influenced by a late classical writer on dreams, Macrobius, as well as by Guillaume de Lorris's *Roman de la Rose.*[56] By the end of the sixteenth century, dreams had become a subject of such interest that one of Shakespeare's contemporaries, Thomas Nashe, felt compelled to debunk the more excessive claims for dreams in *The Terrors of the Night, or a Discourse of Apparitions* (1594). Shakespeare's own spoofing of dreams in *Romeo and Juliet,* as in Mercutio's denigration of them as "children of an idle brain / Begot of nothing but vain fantasy" (1.4.97–98), may owe something to Nashe's dismissal of dreams as "fragments of idle imaginations."[57]

Typically, Shakespeare took a complementary view of dreams,[58] treating them on the one hand seriously, as in Calphurnia's dream or in Hermia's (2.2.151–60), and on the other hand lightly, as in Mercutio's catalogue of dreamers under Queen Mab's influence (*Romeo and Juliet* 1.4.70–88). In *A Midsummer Night's Dream,* this attitude governs the entire play. Or, as Garber puts it,

> *A Midsummer Night's Dream* is a play consciously concerned with dreaming: it reverses the categories of reality and illusion, sleeping and waking, art and nature, to touch upon the central theme of the dream which is truer than reality.

Puck offers the traditional apologia at the play's end; if the audience is dissatisfied, it may choose to regard the play as only a "dream" or trifle and not a real experience at all. The players, as Theseus has already suggested, are only "shadows" (5.1.205); the play, in short, is potentially reducible to a "weak and idle theme" of no significance. Yet everything which has gone before points in precisely the opposite direction: sleep in *A Midsummer Night's Dream* is the gateway, not to folly, but to revelation and reordering; the "visions" gained are, as Bottom says, "most rare" (4.1.200), and the "shadows" substantial. (59–60)

THE SOCIAL MILIEU

Although *A Midsummer Night's Dream* is set in classical Athens, it reflects a good deal of the social life with which Shakespeare and his contemporaries were familiar. In this it resembles many of Shakespeare's other plays which, whatever the setting—Sicily, Venice, Spain—speak directly to Shakespeare's countrymen, his audience in the public theaters and elsewhere. According to Anthony Grafton, *A Midsummer Night's Dream* "presents noblemen and artisans, separated by an enormous difference in wealth and standing but linked by their shared ability to read and write. It reveals that aristocrats and commoners alike were literate enough to use their skills for recreation as well as for practical ends."[59] As noted above, the workmen who rehearse and perform "Pyramus and Thisbe" are right out of Shakespeare's Warwickshire, but the aristocrats that provide the stage audience for the performance reflect the kinds of noblemen and women Shakespeare likely knew from mingling, for example, with the earl of Southampton and his circle. The characters he created in *Love's Labor's Lost* a short while earlier, or in *Much Ado about Nothing* and *As You Like It* a few years later, derive from similar sources.

England in Shakespeare's time was mostly an agrarian society with an agrarian economy. London was by far the largest urban center—one of very few in England. Many of those who populated London came, like Shakespeare, from country towns and villages. Shakespeare could speak to them directly not only through his rude mechanicals, but also through the middle class or gentry represented by Egeus and the young lovers. While upward mobility was difficult and only the most enterprising and able succeeded—again like Shakespeare—interaction among the various classes was commonplace. The population then was very small compared to London's and England's today, or what they were to become by the time Shakespeare was finally laid to rest.[60]

About the time that Shakespeare composed *A Midsummer Night's Dream*, the harvest was so bad that food shortages and resulting high prices posed serious problems. "The maintenance of order and social stability, the provision of an adequate supply of foodstuffs, and the ability to raise money and men to fight wars were the economic and social priorities of the government."[61] *A Midsummer Night's Dream* reflects almost none of these concerns, except for Titania's speech regarding the topsy-turvy world that her quarrel with Theseus has precipitated, with the consequent disruption of the seasons and the damaging effect upon the harvest (2.1.88–100). Not until Shakespeare wrote *Coriolanus* did the economic and social concerns representing real threats to the polity become an important issue at the beginning of that play. *Coriolanus*, however, is a tragedy, and the *Dream* is a comedy, in which such concerns, though real enough and hence not entirely excluded, do not take prominence.

One aspect of social life in Shakespeare's England that is specifically invoked in the *Dream* is the observance of May Day along with the festivities of Midsummer Eve. Chaucer's mention of May Day customs in "The Knight's Tale" may have suggested the connection to Shakespeare.[62] Palamon and Arcite first see Emelye on a May morning, and later Arcite rides to the wood to perform the rite of May. This rite celebrated the arrival of spring with music, singing, dancing, and general frolic. Customs included decorating houses with greenery, especially hawthrone branches, and hanging lights. As C. L. Barber describes it: "The bringing home of May acted out an experience of the relationship between vitality in people and nature."[63] Lysander designates the location where he will meet with Hermia to elope as the place where he once met with Hermia and Helena "To do observance to a morn of May" (1.1.166); and when Theseus comes upon the couples in the woods in act 4, he suspects that they have risen early to "observe the rite of May" (4.1.129–30). The play's title seems to indicate that all the events occur on Midsummer Eve (June 23), not in May, but the custom of Maying was not limited to May Day (May 1), any more than midsummer madness was limited to June 23.[64]

Midsummer Eve was associated with the summer solstice, an ancient holiday honoring the sun. By Shakespeare's time it had become a night of general merriment: bonfires were lit, and the folk gathered medicinal herbs and magical plants. All-night vigils were held, as love rituals and divinations were practiced. Spirits were believed to roam the countryside, and strange events were anticipated. Besides, June was—as it is still— a traditional month for marriages. Shakespeare seems interested in connecting all these associations in his play and in deliberately blurring time signals, as David Young says,

> in order to dismiss calendar time and establish a more elusive festival time. Marriage gives the story its proper comic framework and sense of order. May Day introduces the theme of infatuated love. ... Midsummer Eve ... turns day to night and extends the natural so as to accommodate madness, mystery, and the supernatural in the form of spirits. ... The ambience of festivity is complex and resonant, and it depends for its effectiveness upon the audience's recognition and assent.[65]

Young further argues that, in *A Midsummer Night's Dream*, Shakespeare was trying to improve on his previous four comedies and those of his predecessors by "offering a greater variety of dramatic materials and, consequently, a complexity of possible sources."[66] In this, he was very largely successful.

NOTES

1. Harold Brooks, ed., *A Midsummer Night's Dream* (Arden Shakespeare 2). London: Methuen, 1979, xxxvii.

2. J. Dover Wilson, "Allusions and Occasion," in *A Midsummer Night's Dream*, ed. Arthur Quiller-Couch and John Dover Wilson, 99. Cambridge, England: Cambridge University Press, 1924.

3. E. K. Chambers, *William Shakespeare*. Oxford: Clarendon Press, 1930, 1: 358.

4. This theory was proposed by Wilson in his edition, 91–99.

5. E. K. Chambers, *Shakespearean Gleanings*. Oxford: Oxford University Press, 1944, 61–69.

6. Wilson, "Allusions and Occasion," 100.

7. Brooks, *Midsummer Night's Dream*, 1v–1vi. Brooks favors the Carey-Berkeley wedding held at the mansion of the bride's father, Sir George Carey, in Blackfriars. He admits, however, to the paucity of evidence and the inability to establish the queen's presence.

8. These roles were doubled in Adrian Noble's production of the play for the Royal Shakespeare Company (see chapter 6 of this volume). On the doubling of roles in Shakespeare's company, and particularly in this play, see William Ringler, "The Number of Actors in Shakespeare's Early Plays," in *The*

Seventeenth-Century Stage, ed. G. E. Bentley, 110–34. Chicago: University of Chicago Press, 1968; compare Peter Holland, ed., *A Midsummer Night's Dream*. Oxford: Clarendon Press, 1994, 24.

9. See Stanley Wells, "*A Midsummer Night's Dream* Revisited," *Critical Survey* 3 (1991), 14–29. In *Our Moonlight Revels: "A Midsummer Night's Dream" in the Theatre* (Iowa City: University of Iowa Press, 1997), 1–18, Gary Jay Williams reviews additional events associated with the so-called wedding myth. He concludes, "Testing the wedding-play theory against playhouse practices, I have suggested that plays programmed closely to court occasions would have ill suited a professional company that was primarily dependent for its livelihood on its public playhouse and that moved, probably quickly, between its public and court venues" (p. 18).

10. See *Romeo and Juliet*, 3.5.126–95.

11. Chapter 5, in the translation by Miles Coverdale, another ardent Protestant, who also translated the Bible into English.

12. Ibid. Compare Henry Smith, *A Preparative to Marriage*. London, 1591, 43, who also invokes the commandment in this context.

13. See the note by R. A. Foakes in his edition of *A Midsummer Night's Dream*, New Cambridge Shakespeare. Cambridge, England: Cambridge University Press, 1984, 50.

14. Cited by Holland, *Midsummer Night's Dream*, 22.

15. Earlier, in 1575, an entertainment played before the queen on one of her royal progresses was called "The Queen of the Fayry." Again in 1578, in Churchyard's entertainment performed before her in Norwich, fairies appeared. See Minor White Latham, *The Elizabethan Fairies*. New York: Columbia University Press, 1930, 16. Spenser introduced fairies of a more usual kind in an earlier work, *The Shepheards Calendar* (1579).

16. For the disputes between Catholic and Protestant theologians concerning the origin and nature of fairies, see Gail Kern Paster and Skiles Howard, *A Midsummer Night's Dream: Texts and Contexts*. Boston: Bedford/St. Martin's, 1999, 307–9.

17. See Robert Burton, *The Anatomy of Melancholy*, as cited by Latham, *Elizabethan Fairies*, 26, and compare the reference to Drayton's *Nimphidia* cited by K. M. Briggs, *The Anatomy of Puck: An Examination of Fairy Beliefs Among Shakespeare's Contemporaries and Successors*. London: Routledge and Kegan Paul, 1959, 10–11, 14–15.

18. Although Puck inclines perhaps more to the worse sort of fairy, his malignity is mere mischief, as his introduction at 2.1.32–57 argues, and he does eventually carry out Oberon's beneficent purpose where the young lovers are concerned. For more on Puck, see Carol Rose, *Spirits, Fairies, Leprechauns, and Goblins: An Encyclopedia*. New York: W. W. Norton, 1996, 267.

19. Latham, *Elizabethan Fairies*, 28.

20. Briggs, *Anatomy of Puck*, 14. See also her quotation from the medieval

writer Giraldus Cambrensis, p. 18, on the small but well-formed stature of fairies and their "high character." See also Joan Ozark Holmer, "No 'Vain Fantasy': Shakespeare's Refashioning of Nashe for Dreams and Queen Mab," in *"Romeo and Juliet": Texts, Contexts, and Interpretation*, ed. Jay L. Halio, 49. Newark: University of Delaware Press, 1995. Holmer notes that John Lyly was probably the first to introduce small fairies into Elizabethan drama in *Endimion*, but Shakespeare was the first to couple mortals' dreams with diminutive fairies.

21. Holland, *Midsummer Night's Dream*, 23. Compare Mercutio's description of Queen Mab in *Romeo and Juliet*, 1.4.53–95, and see Ernest Schanzer, "*A Midsummer Night's Dream*," in *Shakespeare: The Comedies*, ed. Kenneth Muir, 30. Englewood Cliffs, N.J.: Prentice-Hall, 1962.

22. Briggs, *Anatomy of Puck*, 9–10.

23. Geoffrey Bullough, *Narrative and Dramatic Sources of Shakespeare's Plays*. New York: Columbia University Press, 1957–75. 1: 370.

24. Ibid. Compare Foakes, *Midsummer Night's Dream*, 6–7.

25. Rose, *Spirits, Fairies*, 309; Bullough, *Narrative and Dramatic Sources*, 371.

26. Bullough, *Narrative and Dramatic Sources*, 371.

27. Foakes, *Midsummer Night's Dream*, 6.

28. Rose, *Spirits, Fairies*, 267.

29. Foakes, *Midsummer Night's Dream*, 7.

30. Bullough, *Narrative and Dramatic Sources*, 371; compare Foakes, *Midsummer Night's Dream*, 7, who argues that Shakespeare need not have read Scot for hints about Puck, since he was well enough known in fairy lore.

31. For other allusions, see Latham, *Elizabethan Fairies*, 177–78.

32. See ibid., 178–218. Compare Briggs, *Anatomy of Puck*, 56–70 (cited by Foakes, *Midsummer Night's Dream*, 8), who argues against Latham that the miniscule size of Shakespeare's fairies (in the fairy train) was not his innovation but has ample precedence in lore and legend (see also K. M. Briggs, *The Fairies in Tradition and Literature*. London: Routledge and Kegan Paul, 1967, 20–21, 88–90). Shakespeare's influence on subsequent literary representations of fairies is nonetheless undeniable.

33. See Bullough's extract from North's Plutarch in *Narrative and Dramatic Sources*, 385–88. Theseus's "faults touching women and ravishments" are described in Plutarch's comparison of Theseus with Romulus, the Roman ruler he parallels, also in Bullough, 388–89.

34. Paster and Howard, *A Midsummer Night's Dream: Texts and Contexts*, 194, 195.

35. Bullough, *Narrative and Dramatic Sources*, 368.

36. See the excerpts from "The Knight's Tale" in Brooks's edition, *Midsummer Night's Dream*, 129–34. Bullough also prints some extracts; see 377–84 of *Narrative and Dramatic Sources*.

37. Bullough, *Narrative and Dramatic Sources*, 369.

38. Holland, *Midsummer Night's Dream*, 69.

39. Ibid., 70, cites this incident and quotes an excerpt from it. His analysis of the tale and its relation to Shakespeare's play (69–73) is full of insights. He rightly argues, for example, with respect to the erotic aspects that Apuleius's tale conveys, that "what is so remarkable about Titania's night with Bottom is not a subdued, suppressed sexual bestiality that has only been properly uncovered in the twentieth century but rather the innocence which transfroms something that might so easily have been full of animal sexuality into something touchingly naive" (73).

40. Bullough, *Narrative and Dramatic Sources*, 397–98, prints an excerpt from the 1573 edition.

41. See ibid., 401–5, for extracts from Cooper and Scot. Scot's emphasis XIII.19, as Holland notes (*Midsummer Night's Dream*, 74), is on apparent transformation, not a true one, depending for effect entirely upon the spectator's vision.

42. Holland, *Midsummer Night's Dream*, 74. On the facing page, Holland reproduces the picture from Brant's *Narrenschiff* of a wheel of fortune showing men being transformed into asses.

43. References are to the reprint in Bullough, *Narrative and Dramatic Sources*, 405–22.

44. Compare *Dream*, 5.1.183–86.

45. At 3.1.18–20, Quince discusses with Bottom the metrical form of his proposed prologue, and they agree on "eight and eight," that is, rhymed lines of eight syllables each. But the prologue (5.1.108–17) is actually in rhymed pentameters, like the playlet that follows, up to line 260.

46. See Jay L. Halio, *Shakespeare in Performance: A Midsummer Night's Dream*. Manchester, England: Manchester University Press, 1994, 65–66. Compare Holland, *Midsummer Night's Dream*, 95.

47. Bullough, *Narrative and Dramatic Sources*, 374. Thomson's poem is reprinted on pp. 409–11.

48. Ibid., 375. Bullough prints the play on pp. 411–22.

49. Ibid., 373.

50. Ibid.

51. Compare Brooks, *Midsummer Night's Dream*, xxxviii: "There is, of course, no compelling reason why learning's decease in beggary should be other than allegorical. The scholar's destitution for want of due patronage was a perennial topic."

52. See Holland, *Midsummer Night's Dream*, 18–19.

53. Technically, a "dream" is something experienced while one is asleep; a "vision" may be had while awake. The *Oxford English Dictionary* fosters the fusion, or confusion, of terms in the definition of *dream* 1.a: "A train of

thoughts, images, or fancies passing through the mind during sleep; a vision during sleep." Compare *vision* 1.a: "Something which is apparently seen otherwise than by ordinary sight."

54. See Marjorie Garber, *Dream in Shakespeare*. New Haven, Conn.: Yale University Press, 1974, 5–8; Holland, *Midsummer Night's Dream*, 5–16.

55. Ibid., 7–8.

56. Ibid., 10–12; Holland, *Midsummer Night's Dream*, 7–8.

57. Holmer, "No 'Vain Fantasy,' " 50.

58. For the concept of complementarity in Shakespeare, see Norman Rabkin, *Shakespeare and the Common Understanding*. New York: Free Press, 1967.

59. Anthony Grafton, "Education and Apprenticeship," in *William Shakespeare: His World, His Work, His Influence*, ed. John F. Andrews, 1: 55. New York: Charles Scribner's Sons, 1985. Volume 1 contains many essays on Shakespeare's "world" (e.g., government and politics under Elizabeth I and James I, law and legal institutions, economic life, manners, dress, and decorum).

60. See D. C. Coleman, "Economic Life in Shakespeare England," in *William Shakespeare: His World, His Work, His Influence*, ed. John F. Andrews, 1: 67–73. New York: Charles Scribner's Sons, 1985.

61. Ibid., 1: 72.

62. David P. Young, *Something of Great Constancy: The Art of "A Midsummer Night's Dream."* New Haven, Conn.: Yale University Press, 1966, 18.

63. C. L. Barber, *Shakespeare's Festive Comedy*. Princeton, N.J.: Princeton University Press, 1959, 18. Cited by Young, *Something of Great Constancy*, 19.

64. Young, *Something of Great Constancy*, 24. Barber says, "The point of the allusions is not the date, but the *kind* of holiday occasion" (120).

65. Ibid. Compare Barber, *Festive Comedy*, 11: "To make a dramatic epithalamium, [Shakespeare] expressed with full imaginative resonance the experience of the traditional summer holidays."

66. Ibid, 33. See also Annabel Patterson, "Bottom's Up: Festive Theory in *A Midsummer Night's Dream*," in *"A Midsummer Night's Dream": Critical Essays*, ed. Dorothea Kehler, 165–78. New York: Garland, 1998.

3

DRAMATIC STRUCTURE

"What sets *A Dream* apart from [Shakespeare's] earlier comedies," Robert Ornstein has stated, "is not so much its richly sensuous and evocative poetry, though that is new to the comedies, as its complex and perfectly assured dramatic structure."[1] The term "dramatic structure," we must remember, is not synonymous with "plot" and must not be confused with it. The plot of *A Midsummer Night's Dream* is multiple, at least fourfold; it concerns Theseus and Hippolyta, the young lovers, Oberon and Titania, and finally Quince and his fellows and their attempt to put on a play. The dramatic structure consists of the ways in which these various plots intersect and interact with other, as they do especially throughout the central scenes of the play.

Another way of approaching the dramatic structure is through an analysis of the planes of reality found in the play. E.M.W. Tillyard uses the term in *Shakespeare's Last Plays*, and S. L. Bethell further develops it in *Shakespeare and the Popular Dramatic Tradition*.[2] Briefly stated, the term refers to the different modes of existence which individuals may perceive in others or find in themselves. Shakespeare was fully aware of the different planes of reality accessible to human consciousness, as for example when he has Fabian comment in *Twelfth Night* on Malvolio's appearance before Olivia, cross-gartered in yellow stockings: "If this were played upon a stage now, I would condemn it as an improbable fiction" (3.4.127–28).[3] The comment reminds the audience that they are in fact watching a play, which is of a different order of reality from their everyday life. Cleopatra invokes a similar contrast when she fears that if she allows Octavius to capture her, "Some squeaking Cleopatra [will] boy my greatness / I' the posture of a whore" (*Antony and Cleopatra*, 5.2.219–20).[4] Comments of this kind elicit from the audience a form of multiconsciousness[5] that is essential to the full apprehension of Shakespeare's dramatic action.

Bethell suggests that different poetic styles may signal different planes of reality. Using examples from *As You Like It*, he suggests that "Shakespeare is . . . careful . . . to indicate through his verse-technique the varying degrees of actuality to which we are expected to adjust ourselves" (35–36). This is as true of the complexity of *A Midsummer Night's Dream* as it is of his later pastoral play. Compare, for example—to cite one of the most striking contrasts—the difference between Bottom's speech in his encounter with Titania in the forest and hers. The difference is more than that between blank verse and prose:

> *Titania* I pray thee, gentle mortal, sing again;
> Mine ear is much enamoured of thy note.
> So is mine eye enthrallèd to thy shape,
> And thy fair virtue's force perforce doth move me
> On the first view to say, to swear, I love thee.
>
> *Bottom* Methinks, mistress, you should have little reason
> for that. And yet, to say the truth, reason and love keep little company together nowadays; the more the pity that some honest neighbours will not make them friends. Nay, I can gleek upon occasion.
> (3.1.114–22)

Bottom's simple, homespun language along with his mother wit contrasts directly with Titania's elegant, courtly idiom—a contrast that continues throughout the play, not only between these two characters, but also between the rude mechanicals and the courtiers in Theseus's court. The contrast helps to define for the audience the difference between the realms of existence that they inhabit, as much as—or perhaps more than—the costumes they wear.

The contrast is not so striking between Theseus and Hippolyta, on the one hand, and Oberon and Titania, on the other. Both sets of characters, after all, are royalty, though royalty of a different kind. That being the case, perhaps a sharp eye, or rather ear, should be able to distinguish between their speech patterns, even though these characters never meet or interact as Bottom and Titania do. Still, they represent different planes of reality. Compare, for instance, the more rational-minded Theseus's idiom with that of the more romantic or otherwordly Oberon:

Theseus What say you, Hermia? Be advised, fair maid.
To you your father should be as a god,
One that composed your beauties; yea, and one
To whom you are but as a form in wax
By him imprinted, and within his power
To leave the figure, or disfigure it.
Demetrius is a worthy gentleman. (1.1.46–52)

Oberon I know a bank where the wild thyme blows,
Where oxlips and the nodding violet grows,
Quite overcanopied with luscious woodbine,
With sweet musk-roses, and with eglantine:
There sleeps Titania sometime of the night,
Lulled in these flowers with dances and delight;
And there the snake throws her enamelled skin,
Weed wide enough to wrap a fairy in. (2.1.249–56)

The contrast here involves much more than the contrast between blank verse and rhymed couplets. Theseus employs simile but mainly to impress on Hermia the conventional advice he gives her. Oberon uses metaphor in a rich verbal description imaging Titania's bower—the kind of poetry that later Theseus disdains in his description of the poet in his speech on the imagination at the beginning of act 5.

There is little or nothing in the speech of the four lovers to distinguish among them, nor is there any need, as they come from the same social stratum, are of the same age, and have the same basic interests. The contrast is rather with Puck's speech and that of the other fairies, who are of a different order of reality altogether. Shakespeare makes the contrast impossible to miss, partly by his varied use of meter and rhyme:

Puck Captain of our fairy band,
Helena is here at hand,
And the youth mistook by me,
Pleading for a lover's fee.
Shall we their fond pageant see?
Lord, what fools these mortals be! (3.2.110–15)

Lysander Why should you think that I should woo in scorn?
Scorn and derision never come in tears.
Look when I vow, I weep; and vows so born,
In their nativity all truth appears.

> How can these things in me seem scorn to you,
> Bearing the badge of faith to prove them true? (3.2.122–27)

Puck is quick and to the point, relishing the prospect of mischief. Lysander is the distraught lover, full of sententiousness and pleading. Helena, rejecting him, speaks in similar idiom. A few lines later, when Demetrius awakes, he too speaks in their idiom, blinded like Lysander by the magic love potion and professing his love for Helena just as strenuously.

Finally, the play-within-the-play contrasts with everything that has gone before (except for Bottom's earlier speech in "Ercles' vein," 1.2.24–31). Shakespeare here meant to set off the play world of the action proper from the play world of "Pyramus and Thisbe," using an archaic verse mode and an acting style to match it, as he later did in *Hamlet* in "The Murder of Gonzago."

Style, including verse technique, is then one of the ways in which the worlds of *A Midsummer Night's Dream* are distinguished,[6] but now we need to look more closely into other aspects of these worlds, specifically the ways in which they intersect and in so doing help to complicate and develop the dramatic structure of the play.

A Midsummer Night's Dream opens in the classical Athens of Theseus's court, and it ends there. Within this frame, all of the other action of the play takes place. Theseus bemoans the wait he must endure before he can consummate his love for Hippolyta, but she sensibly reassures him that the time will pass quickly:

> Four days will quickly steep themselves in night;
> Four nights will quickly dream away the time;
> And then the moon, like a silver bow
> New bent in heaven, shall behold the night
> Of our solemnities (1.1.6–11)

If the time frame of the play is calculated from the action that ensues, fewer than four days and nights pass before the wedding celebration actually occurs, but in the theater such a literal calculation is irrelevant. By act 5, when the weddings have taken place and the celebrations proceed, no one remembers the "four nights" or has counted the days that have passed. Time here, as elsewhere in Shakespeare's plays, is fluid and needs to be measured more in terms of Bergsonian *durée* than chronometrical days and hours; that is, time as lived experience as opposed to clocked time.[7]

Theseus's court is the center, nevertheless, of practical reason. When Egeus intrudes moments after Theseus promises his bride that he will wed her in a key different from the way he wooed her, a contretemps breaks out between Hermia and her father that Theseus must resolve. Egeus invokes the law of Athens, which Theseus feels compelled to enforce. Hippolyta's silence while all this goes on is often taken as a sign of her displeasure, though no explicit reference in the text supports this interpretation. Theseus at length invites Egeus and Demetrius to withdraw to confer with him on "something nearly that concerns your-selves" (1.1.125). It is clearly his means to allow Lysander and Hermia time to consider their situation under the conditions that he has laid down.

Consider it they do. Lysander comes up with a scheme to elope, to which Hermia agrees. When Helena enters, we recall that she was once beloved of Demetrius, but now she is terribly unhappy—the more so since her best friend Hermia is currently the object of Demetrius's af-fection. Pleading with Hermia to tell her how to look and act so that Demetrius will return her affection, Helena unwittingly anticipates the action of the forest scenes, when both Demetrius and Lysander will sue for her hand. Taking pity on Helena, Hermia and Lysander confide in Helena and reveal their secret to elope. This gives Helena an opportunity to gain at least a modicum of appreciation from Demetrius by disclosing the plan to him.

The world of the four lovers stands in direct contrast to the calm and orderly world of the older couple, Theseus and Hippolyta. Whatever their struggles once were, they have apparently resolved them satisfactorily and now look forward to a life together as husband and wife—not so the world of the fairy king and queen, whom we meet that night in the next act. Their world—and with it the world of nature—has been badly fractured by their ongoing quarrel over the little Indian prince that Titania has and Oberon desires. If the world of Theseus and Hippolyta is ruled by reason, high passion dominates the fairy kingdom—and with dire consequences, as the speeches of Oberon and Titania clearly indicate. Consider, for example, Titania's reply to Oberon's criticism of her dal-liance with Theseus:

> These are the forgeries of jealousy:
> And never since the middle summer's spring

> Met we on hill, in dale, forest, or mead,
> By pavèd fountain or by rushy brook,
> Or in the beachèd margent of the sea
> To dance our ringlets to the whistling wind,
> But with thy brawls thou hast disturbed our sport.
> Therefore the winds, piping to us in vain,
> As in revenge have sucked up from the sea
> Contagious fogs; which, falling in the land,
> Hath every pelting river made so proud
> That they have overcome their continents.
> The ox hath therefore stretched his yoke in vain,
> The ploughman lost his sweat, and the green corn
> Hath rotted ere his youth attained a beard.
> The fold stands empty in the drownèd field. (2.1.81–96)

She continues in this vein, piling example upon example, alluding to the moon, "Pale in her anger," as her own anger rises. Oberon expresses his anger not so much in words here as in action: his plan is to teach Titania a lesson regarding obedience to her lord and master. Hence, he sends Puck to find the magic flower, love-in-idleness, whose juice will propel Titania into the most hateful predicament she has ever known.

Between this episode and the first, however, Shakespeare inserted the first scene with Peter Quince and his fellows. They gather in preparation to rehearse a play they hope to perform before the duke and his bride on their wedding night. If the world of Theseus's court represents an elevated and sophisticated society, and fairyland represents an even loftier but much more mysterious world, these yokels present a very basic, workaday world of simple aspirations. The contrasts with 1.1 and 2.1 could hardly be greater, and that may indeed be Shakespeare's point in establishing the multiple planes of reality in this play. For we recall that in Elizabethan drama, the scene was the basic dramatic unit used, as here, in juxtaposition with scenes before and after to provide significant comparisons and contrasts. Quince and his friends, far from being denizens of classical Athens, come straight from Shakespeare's Warwickshire, provoking his audience into the kind of multiconsciousness that his complex drama requires. For if the imagination can accept a world of the fairy in the forest outside Athens, why not also a group of English workmen within the confines of the city? Shakespeare has further purposes for this little band of amateur thespians, as we shall see.

After Titania departs from Oberon in 2.1, leaving him to his own devices, Demetrius and Helena enter the forest. Like 1.1, 2.1 is a portmanteau scene; that is, it is a scene that contains several different but continuous actions, or segments, connected by one or more characters remaining on stage.[8] The quarrel between Demetrius and Helena parallels that between Oberon and Titania, though its substance is different. Helena pursues Demetrius into the forest, both searching for Lysander and Hermia; or rather, Demetrius is searching for Hermia and trying to get rid of Helena, who has informed him of the elopement, and her abject pleading for him to love her. It is in many ways a scene of comic pathos. Oberon, standing by, takes pity on the poor woman, revealing that he can also be a compassionate individual and not altogether the hard-hearted, domineering man who is plotting against his queen. Although neither Demetrius nor Helena can see him—he makes himself invisible[9]—he overhears all of their dialogue and promises that before Demetrius leaves the forest, Helena will flee from him and he will pursue her.

Puck returns with the magic flower, and after telling him what he is going to do to Titania, Oberon instructs Puck to seek out the Athenian youth who has disdained the woman who loves him. He tells Puck that he will know the man "By the Athenian garments he hath on" (2.1.264). Little does he or Puck know that another Athenian youth is also in the forest, and this lack of knowledge leads to the confusions that delight Puck later and upset Oberon.

The next scene shows Titania among her fairies in the bower Oberon has already described (2.1.249–56). The action starts as a lovely interlude of peacefulness and beauty. After beckoning her fairies to sing her to sleep, Titania drowses off while listening to their lullaby. The lines are supposed to act as a charm to ward off any noxious creatures that might harm the fairy queen; however, neither Titania nor her fairies suspect that Oberon lies in wait for just this moment to place the magic potion on her eyelids. The first thing that she sees upon awakening—"Be it ounce or cat or bear, / Pard or boar with bristled hair" (2.2.36–37)—will become the object of her uncontrollable infatuation.

Oberon exits, and Lysander and Hermia enter. (This is yet another portmanteau scene.) They are quite lost, as Lysander admits, and weary with trying to find their way. They are utterly unaware that they are in fairyland, quite close to Titania's bower, which apparently they do not or cannot see.[10] They decide to rest until morning, and after a little love play, during which Hermia demurely and chastely insists that Lysander lie some distance away from her, they both fall asleep. Puck enters, and spying an Athenian, he puts the love potion on Lysander's eyes. He does

not realize that this is the wrong Athenian; after all, he has been searching up and down the forest trying to carry out his master's orders. He
is naturally relieved, therefore, to find the man he thinks is he who
"Despisèd the Athenian maid" and not far from him the maiden herself
"sleeping sound / On the dank and dirty ground" (2.2.79–81).

When Puck leaves, Demetrius and Helena again enter. She is still
chasing after him, but by now is much too tired to continue. When he
leaves, Helena goes into another of her laments, comparing herself un-
favorably to Hermia, until she suddenly sees Lysander lying on the
ground nearby. Unsure whether he is alive or dead, and failing to see
Hermia, she says, "Lysander, if you live, good sir, awake!" (2.2.107).
He does and startles her with his profuse declaration of love: "And run
through fire for thy sweet sake!" (108). Helena is amazed, then angry,
believing that he is mocking her and is not at all sincere. Insulted, she
leaves, complaining, "O, that a lady of one man refused / Should of
another therefore be abused!" (139–40).

Undaunted, Lysander runs after her, bidding the still sleeping Hermia
the unkindest farewell; whereupon Hermia awakens, crying out for Lysander. She has had a terrible nightmare, imagining a "crawling serpent"
eating her heart away while he sat smiling at the sight (2.2.151–56). The
symbolism is obvious enough. Surprised that Lysander is nowhere in
view and now thoroughly frightened, Hermia determines to find him or
die in the attempt (157–62). Thus begins the compounding of confusions
that reaches its climax in 3.2.

The scene now returns to Peter Quince & Co., who have entered the
forest to rehearse their play. They chose to go there so that rival towns-
folk would not see what they are up to (1.2.80–82). Shakespeare, of
course, has another purpose in mind: the trick that Puck will play on
Nick Bottom and the complications that arise when Titania awakens and
sees him. In the meantime, the men begin considering how they will
perform their play of Pyramus and Thisbe. Bottom's concern for the
effect on the ladies in the audience when Pyramus kills himself also
arouses the consternation of others in the troupe. But instead of omitting
the action, as Starveling suggests, Bottom comes up with a different
solution: Quince will write a prologue to explain everything; that is,
Pyramus is not really killed, and in fact neither is he Pyramus, but Bottom the weaver (3.1.12–17). This explanation, he is sure, will erase any
fear that might otherwise ensue.

Here as later, when they ponder the problem of the lion's roaring and
bringing moonlight into the court chamber, the mechanicals reveal their

literal mindedness as regards acting and dramatic performance in general. Shakespeare doubtless included it as another way of evoking audience consciousness about the nature and function of drama. As the audience becomes aware of what Bottom and the others worry about, they also become aware of what they are watching—Shakespeare's *A Midsummer Night's Dream*. It is another means employed by Shakespeare to arouse multiconsciousness, here of the different modes of reality that play performance involves. In point of fact, Quince never delivers the prologue that Bottom suggests; instead, he offers a rather different one, once their play is preferred; but that is irrelevant to the issue Shakespeare deals with in this part of the scene.

The next part begins as the men start their rehearsal and Puck enters. Amused by what he sees, Puck decides to indulge his inclination to mischief. While Bottom is offstage awaiting his cue to reenter after Thisbe finishes her lines, Puck transforms the unsuspecting weaver into a grotesque image with an ass's head. His reappearance is accordingly astonishing. It frightens Quince and all the others, who dash about madly trying to escape the horrific vision before them. Unaware of what they see, and believing it is just a trick they are playing on him to make him afraid (3.1.94–102), Bottom walks up and down and sings a tune to himself. His singing awakens the fairy queen, who has been lying in her bower while all this has been going on. Just as the magic potion affected Lysander when he awoke and saw Helena, so it affects Titania when she awakes and sees Bottom with his ass's head: "What angel wakes me from my flowery bed?" (3.1.107), she asks, as Bottom goes on singing his rustic tune.

Not hearing or seeing her, or ignoring what he cannot believe he sees, Bottom continues singing his raucous song about birds cuckolded by the cuckoo, as Oberon, ironically, will soon be cuckolded by Bottom. Titania persists, again like Lysander, begging Bottom to "sing again" (3.1.113). Her ear is as enamored of him as are her eyes, and she professes her love for him. Responding to her at last, Bottom replies in matter-of-fact tones, remarking on one of the play's major themes: "to say the truth, reason and love keep little company together nowadays" (120–21). To which Titania replies, "Thou art as wise as thou art beautiful" (123).

To his credit, Bottom is not impressed by Titania's flattery. If he were truly wise, he says, he would know how to get out of this forest. Here, as later on, Bottom shows his mother wit, which appeals to the audience as much as, or perhaps more than, his person appeals to the benighted Titania. The fairy queen will hear nothing of his desire to escape from the woods—and her. She promises him jewels and pleasures undreamed of and calls on her fairies to be "kind and courteous to this gentleman" (3.1.142) and to minister to his every need—all in some of the loveliest and most beguiling verses ever written by Shakespeare. And so they do; and as they do, Bottom greets them in turn—Cobweb, Peaseblossom, Mustardseed—with the simple recognition of their several virtues and his own kind of homely courtesy. Powerless to resist or protest, Bottom is led away while Titania comments on the moon that looks "with a watery eye" on every little flower lamenting on "some enforcèd chastity" (175–77). Bottom's chastity will not be enforced, however; quite the opposite is in store for him.

While all this is going on, Oberon in 3.2 wonders what effect his trick is having on Titania. Puck enters and tells him, expanding at length on how he transformed Bottom and what has happened not only to Titania but also to his fellows (3.2.6–34). The speech is Shakespeare's stage direction for how 3.1.86–98 should be played.[11] Delighted at this success, Oberon inquires about the other use of the flower's charm. No sooner does Puck tell him that he did as directed than Demetrius and Hermia enter, and Puck's mistake stands revealed. Just as Helena rejects Lysander's professions of love, here Hermia rebukes Demetrius and worries that he may have done Lysander some harm. She cannot believe anything else would have caused her lover to abandon her. Demetrius truthfully answers that he is "not guilty of Lysander's blood" (3.2.75), does not know if Lysander is alive or dead, and couldn't care less. Fed up with Demetrius, Hermia leaves him with a stinging rebuke, whereupon Demetrius realizes there is no point in pursuing her in this mood. Besides, he is worn out and lies down to sleep awhile.

This gives Oberon the opportunity to begin to set things right among the four young lovers. Puck's "misprision" (i.e., his error) has resulted in "Some true love turned, and not a false turned true" (3.2.91). Puck cynically remarks that fate lies behind it all, that for every man that remains true in love, "A million fail, confounding oath on oath" (92); this does not impress Oberon. He commands Puck to find Helena, "All fancy-sick . . . and pale of cheer" (95) and bring her while he puts the charm on Demetrius's eyes. This action, he believes, will solve the problem Puck's mistake has caused, but he is unaware that further confusion worse confounded will occur until Lysander's eyes finally receive their antidote.

Puck quickly returns leading Helena, pursued by Lysander. He asks Oberon to watch the "fond pageant" that will follow and comments,

"Lord, what fools these mortals be!" (3.2.115). It is a very foolish pageant indeed, as "two at once woo one," delighting Puck, who is best pleased when things fall out "preposterously." So they do in part during the following action, which presents the comic spectacle of Lysander pursuing Helena pusuing Demetrius pursuing Hermia pursuing Lysander—until, that is, Demetrius awakens, and he too pursues Helena.

To Helena, all this appears as a cruel joke on her. She even comes to believe, after Hermia enters at 3.2.176, that her erstwhile close friend is also in on the joke. The two men, never friendly, now become incensed at each other and are about to come to serious blows until Puck, under Oberon's orders, overcasts the night sufficiently that they cannot find each other in the fog and grow tired with trying. Meanwhile, Hermia and Helena also have at it, calling each other names and hurling bitter accusations one against the other (323–28, 339–44). Oberon further instructs Puck to place the antidote on Lysander's eyes once he is asleep so that when the four lovers awake, "all this derision / Shall seem a dream and fruitless vision" (370–71), and they can all return to Athens "With league whose date till death shall never end" (373). Puck carries out his master's orders during the rest of the scene, leading the young people around and around until all four droop with fatigue and fall asleep. As he squeezes the antidote on Lysander's eyes, he promises that when Lysander awakens he will take "True delight / In the sight / Of [his] former lady's eye; / . . . Jack shall have Jill, / Naught shall go ill: / The man shall have his mare again, and all shall be well" (455–63).

This scene effectively concludes the young lovers' action, except for their discovery by Theseus and the others the next morning as they lie sleeping. Oberon's plot against Titania, suspended at the end of 3.1, still requires closure, which comes in 4.1. Oberon has not yet accomplished what he set out to do, that is, get the Indian boy away from her, and only when that happens will he "her charmèd eye release / From monster's view, and all things shall be peace" (3.2.375–76). Puck warns Oberon that he had better hurry, since night is going fast and dawn approaches. Oberon reassures him, or rather the audience, that they are not like ghosts or demons but "spirits of another sort" (388): they are not evil or harmful to human beings, as indeed his actions concerning the young lovers already has proved. Nevertheless, he senses some urgency, and he agrees that haste is in order.

In Titania's bower (4.1), the fairies, watched by Oberon, treat Bottom just as their mistress has ordered them to do. Becoming accustomed to this treatment, Bottom orders Cobweb to fetch him some honey, and

Mustardseed and Peaseblossom to scratch his ears, which itch. When Titania offers him music, he shows his true heritage and calls for the tongs and bones (4.1.26–27). Offered food, he confesses "a great desire to a bottle of hay" (30). Growing weary, he falls asleep in Titania's arms, as she cries out, "O, how I love thee! How I dote on thee!" (42),[12] until she too falls asleep.

When Puck arrives after carrying out his master's orders, Oberon shows him the grotesque sight before them and says that he has begun to pity his queen. Shakespeare did not dramatize how Oberon obtained the Indian boy; Oberon describes the event to Puck (4.1.45–58), thus avoiding some unnecessary and perhaps clumsy action.[13] Oberon can now release Titania from the "hateful imperfection of her eyes" (60). Puck can also restore Bottom to his proper self, letting him return to Athens like the others of his troupe. The "fierce vexation" of the dream is over for all those who have been afflicted by Oberon's magic (except, of course, Demetrius), and harmony soon resumes sway. Thus, when Titania awakens at Oberon's behest, they are once again a loving couple. Their reconciliation is signaled by the music that Oberon asks Titania to call forth and by the dance that they then perform together—music and dance being the symbols, as elsewhere in Shakespeare, of sweet harmony.

As morning breaks, the fairies all disappear, and Theseus, Hippolyta, and their train, who are out hunting, enter. Theseus brags about the music of his hounds (4.1.103), and Hippolyta recalls how she heard Spartan hounds baying when she was with Hercules and Cadmus once in Crete. She remarks how she had never heard "So musical a discord, such sweet thunder" (115). Theseus claims that his hounds are also of the Spartan kind, "matched in mouth like bells, / Each under each. A cry more tuneable / Was never halooed to nor cheered with horn" (120–22). These oxymorons of concord within discord and sweet thunder comment upon and complement the preceding actions overseen by Oberon. They also lead directly to the discovery of the young lovers who are lying on the ground where Puck had left them.

Questioned by Theseus about how and why they got there, but more particularly "How comes this gentle concord in the world" (4.1.140), where not long before hatred and jealousy ruled, Lysander begins to reply. He tries to explain how he came hither with Hermia to escape "the peril of Athenian law" (150), but before he gets very far, Egeus interrupts him and demands "the law upon his head!" (152). Demetrius then interposes his explanation of events, mentioning how he followed

Hermia and Lysander into the woods with Helena following him. Significantly, he says that he does not know by what power it is, but some power certainly caused his love for Hermia to melt away, to be replaced by his renewed love for Helena. Although he wants to hear more about it, Theseus has heard enough to overbear Egeus's will and declares that the couples will be wed along with Hippolyta and himself "by and by" at the temple in Athens. In this manner, Theseus seals the concord of this discord, silencing Egeus and leaving the couples to wonder at their situation and follow the duke's command to join him and Hippolyta in wedding celebrations.

The scene (yet another portmanteau scene) does not end there, however. One more "dreamer" still has to awake. As he does, Bottom calls out to his fellows for his cue, suddenly realizes he is alone, and begins to wonder, like the young lovers immediately before him, at his "rare vision" (4.1.200). As further evidence of his wit, he knows better than to try to "expound" his dream. Instead, he decides to get Peter Quince to write a ballad of his dream, which "hath no bottom" (208–9), and which he will sing, perhaps, before the duke at the end of a play "at her [Thisbe's] death" (210–11). Like the explanatory prologue he asked Quince to write earlier, however, the ballad never appears.

The next scene is mainly transitional, allowing time for the characters who have entered the woods to return to Athens and prepare for their festivities. Quince and his friends are depressed by Bottom's disappearance and feel certain he has been "transported" (4.2.2). Their hopes for putting on a play before the duke, and the rewards they hope to gain thereby, seem dashed, when all of a sudden Bottom enters and announces that their play is preferred. Overjoyed at his reappearance and the news he brings with him, the group now must get ready for their performance.

At the beginning of act 5, Theseus and Hippolyta are musing upon the story that the lovers have apparently told them about their adventures in the forest. Rational Theseus lectures his bride on "these fairy toys," the caprices of the imagination which make him laugh. This is Shakespeare's means of putting not only the events of acts 2–4 into a certain perspective, but the whole enterprise of poetic creativity. Theseus is not entirely convincing, since Hippolyta replies that there is more to "all the story of the night, / And all their minds transfigured so together" than his explanation of "fancy," or the imagination, can account for. Before they can pursue the discussion further, however, the lovers themselves enter.

Theseus calls on his master of revels, Philostrate, to announce the proposed entertainments for the evening. Philostrate does so, and Theseus rejects first one and then another of the possibilities, with good reason, until he comes to "A tedious brief scene of young Pyramus / And his love Thisbe, very tragical mirth" (5.1.56–57). Amused by these oxymorons—"Merry and tragical"—he wonders how to find the concord of this new discord. Philostrate tries to dissuade him from going forward with it but to no avail. Apparently, Theseus is impressed that the players who aspire to perform before him are precisely the "Hard-handed men that work in Athens here" which Philostrate tells him (72–75).

Showing her humanity in her concern for the workmen's capabilities, Hippolyta says she does not like "to see wretchedness o'ercharged, / And duty in his service perishing" (5.1.85). By that she means she does not anticipate with any pleasure the crude attempts of these poor workmen to put on a play and their attempts failing. Theseus reassures her: "Love . . . and tongue-tied simplicity / In least speak most, to my capacity" (104–5). Later, as the play proceeds, Hippolyta complains that it is "the silliest stuff that ever I heard" (204). Theseus replies, "The best in this kind are but shadows; and the worst are no worse, if imagination mend them" (205–6). Evidently a seasoned playgoer, Theseus has the proper attitude toward stage performance; more to the point, Shakespeare introduced this bit of dialogue as a defense against negative criticism, or to inject his own theory of dramatic performance and its relation to the audience's imagination, on which the actors must invariably depend.[14] Together with his comments on the poetic imagination at the beginning of this scene, Theseus shows himself to be an astute theoretician as well as a humanitarian.

Another issue underlies the inclusion of the play-within-the-play, one that concerns its choice of subject for presentation at this point in the drama. Why present a play about Pyramus and Thisbe? Granted the naive pretentiousness of the mechanicals who perform it, and the farcical manner of their presentation, which evokes laughter from both the stage and the theater audience, could Shakespeare have had another reason for this particular subject? Was his purpose merely to provide a rollicking comedy for everyone's amusement?

In the first place, despite its manner of presentation and its designation, however inept (or not so inept) as "very tragical mirth," the play is a tragedy. But why introduce a tragedy here? Was Shakespeare simply poking fun at his own tragedy of *Romeo and Juliet*, as some scholars believe,[15] assuming that composition of *A Midsummer Night's Dream* followed shortly afterward? I think the answer lies deeper than that and relates very closely to the earlier events in the forest. The tragedy of Pyramus and Thisbe—and even Philostrate concedes that it is a tragedy (5.1.66)—contrasts directly with the fate of the young lovers in the forest. What befell the lovers in Ovid's story could very well have befallen the young Athenians, as Shakespeare seems to remind his audience. Why did it not? Why do Pyramus and Thisbe come to grief and not these lovers?

The answer of course is that Oberon was there in the forest watching over them. He is the providence of the play, the supernatural agent who overlooks the lovers. No such providence oversees the elopement of Pyramus and Thisbe. That is one of the basic differences between comedy and tragedy, between Dante's *Divine Comedy*, say, and Shakespeare's *King Lear*; between the intervention of a caring providential agency and an absent or indifferent one. This is not to dismiss the other contrast, mentioned above, between the archaic style of the playlet and Shakespeare's dramatic style, which helps set it off. Shakespeare often had more than one motive in organizing the structure of his drama.[16]

During the course of the play, everyone seems to have a good time: the actors comporting themselves as well as they can, the stage audience making fun of some of their amateurish enactments, and the actors doing their best to reassure them. Many of the asides spoken by Theseus and the others are probably not heard by the actors as they perform, or they fail to grasp the mockery altogether. In any event, once the play is over, Bottom offers to present their epilogue or a Bergomask dance. Theseus's rejection of the epilogue is interesting in a number of ways:

> No epilogue, I pray you; for your play needs no excuse. Never excuse; for when the players are all dead, there need none to be blamed. Marry, if he that writ it had played Pyramus and hanged himself in Thisbe's garter, it would have been a fine tragedy: and so it is, truly, and very notably discharged. But come, your Bergomask; let your epilogue alone. (5.1.335–37)

Theseus is being very courtly as well as witty; however, since many of Shakespeare's plays end with an epilogue, as this one does, he is hardly Shakespeare's surrogate. For another kind of play than Quince's "Pyramus and Thisbe," an epilogue may well serve, although the injunction, "Never excuse," is well put, and Shakespeare's epilogues seldom excuse. They serve a rather different function.

The Bergomask is something else again, and Theseus welcomes this form of entertainment with which to conclude the evening's revels. A rollicking, high-spirited dance, it is yet one more indication of harmony, here between the lower class mechanicals and the duke and his courtiers. As the clock tolls midnight, Theseus bids the lovers goodnight: " 'tis almost fairy time" (5.1.342). He promises a fortnight of revels and "new jollity" (348), and then all exeunt.

The play does not end there, for it is fairy time indeed. Puck enters carrying a broom and sets the stage for the final entrance of Oberon, Titania, and their train. They come to "sing and bless this place" (5.1.378), as Titania says; hence, Oberon orders each fairy to "take his gait, / And each several chamber bless / Through this palace with sweet peace" (394–96). Finally, after all leave, Puck remains to speak his epilogue, through which Shakespeare once again reminds the audience of the nature of dramatic performance and its relation to commonplace reality, putting both into perspective:

> If we shadows have offended,
> Think but this, and all is mended:
> That you have but slumbered here
> While these visions did appear;
> And this weak and idle theme,
> No more yielding than a dream. (401–6)

To the various planes of reality that Shakespeare dramatized at the end of *A Midsummer Night's Dream* he added one more: the planes of reality that can distinguish between the play world and the world of the audience's ordinary existence.

NOTES

1. Robert Ornstein, *Shakespeare's Comedies*. Newark: University of Delaware Press, 1986, 74. According to Ornstein, "The earlier comedies expand the dimensions of Roman farce by mingling clowns and caricatures with romantic heroes and heroines. *A Dream* has the expansiveness of the later comedies that is created by the presence of multiple dramatic worlds."

2. E.M.W. Tillyard, *Shakespeare's Last Plays*. London: Chatto and Windus, 1938, ch. 3; S. L. Bethell, *Shakespeare and the Popular Dramatic Tradition*. London: Staples Press, 1944, ch. 2.

3. Cited by Bethell, *Shakespeare*, 33.

4. Ibid., 39.

5. See ibid., 81, 108–36 for the use of this term.

6. Compare David P. Young, *Something of Great Constancy: The Art of "A Midsummer Night's Dream,"* New Haven, Conn.: Yale University Press, 1966, 66:

> In addition to individual characterizations, the various meters and rhymes serve to define the groupings in *A Midsummer Night's Dream*. Thus, although the usage is by no means strict, we associate blank verse with Theseus, Hippolyta, and the courtly world at Athens; couplets with the lovers, especially as they move into the woods; lyrical measures, including song and dance, with the fairy world; and prose with the mechanicals, despite their attempts at formal verse. As various groups occupy the center of attention, we hear the particular style associated with them.

On pp. 91–92, Young analyzes the four worlds of the play as a series of concentric circles, with the mechanicals at the inmost circle, the lovers at the next, then the circle of Theseus and Hippolyta, followed by that of the fairies, with the farthest circle belonging to the audience and possibly beyond that one belonging to the playwright, overseeing all. My analysis of the worlds of play parallels Young's, imagining planes or levels of reality instead of concentric circles.

7. See Jay L. Halio, " 'No Clock in the Forest': Time in *As You Like It*," *SEL* 2 (1962), 197–207; and compare G. L. Kittredge: "We need only observe that the four days and four nights contemplated by Hippolita . . . are not fully spanned. . . . No audience would not [*sic*] the discrepancy, for the night in the enchanted forest is long enough to bewilder the imagination" (cited by Young, *Something of Great Constancy*, 86–87).

8. Classical drama, instead, calls for a new scene every time a new major character or characters enters or leaves. Hence, 1.1 would be divided at lines 20, 127, 179, 226; 2.1 at lines 59, 145, 187, 244.

9. In Elizabethan dramatic convention, if a character assumes a disguise, it is regarded as impenetrable. In a sense, invisibility is the disguise Oberon adopts at this time. Although he remains invisible to the mortals he watches, he is of course in plain sight of the audience.

10. In many modern productions, Titania lies asleep on a couch or hammock that is lifted high above the stage. On the Elizabethan stage, she probably lay within the inner stage curtained off from the rest of the action until she is awakened at 3.1.107. See R. A. Foakes, ed., *A Midsummer Night's Dream*. Cambridge, England: Cambridge University Press, 1984, notes to 2.2.30SD and 3.1.107.

11. Shakespeare often imbeds in his dialogue directions of this sort. See Ann Pasternak Slater, *Shakespeare, the Director*. Brighton, England: Harvester Press, 1982.

12. In some modern productions, Titania's lines here and earlier are taken as justification to show her engaging in intercourse with Bottom, but the text hardly

warrants that extreme action. Bottom may cuckold Oberon symbolically, but not necessarily otherwise. Compare Ornstein, *Shakespeare's Comedies*, "Bottom is instinctively chivalric toward women: modest, tactful, thankful for small favors, he would not think of taking advantage of Titania's infatuation. . . . Inevitably he is friendly rather than amorous" (86).

13. Compare Ornstein, *Shakespeare's Comedies*, "If this encounter [between Oberon and Titania] were staged, it might leave an unpleasant aftertaste, but it is reported to us as a conclusion to a marital dispute that ends, as so many do, without explicit resolutions of issues and with unspoken recognitions" (86).

14. Compare the Prologue in *Henry V*, 23–25, 28, which asks the audience to "Piece out our imperfections with your thoughts" and to use "imaginary puissance." See C. L. Barber, *Shakespeare's Festive Comedy*. Princeton, N.J.: Princeton University Press, 1959, 150, n. 22, and chapter 4 of this volume.

15. See, e.g., ibid., 152, and Barber's long note 26. Compare Foakes, *Midsummer Night's Dream*, 2.

16. Compare Alexander Leggatt, *Shakespeare's Comedy of Love*. London: Methuen, 1974, 100: "Despite Philostrate's misgivings, this proves to be the ideal entertainment for a nuptial: the dangers that threaten love are systematically destroyed by the way they are presented."

4

THEMES

Love in a variety of forms is the central theme of *A Midsummer Night's Dream*, but like other of Shakespeare's plays, the *Dream* develops many themes including such diverse topics as the art of stage performance, reality and illusion, reason versus passion, law and authority, friendship, and concord out of discord. This chapter will treat a number of these themes and at the same time attempt to show when and how they are interrelated.

ROMANTIC, MATURE, AND MARRIED LOVE

A character in one of Saul Bellow's novels sees love "as possibly the highest blessing of mankind. A human soul devoid of longing," he says, "was a soul deformed, deprived of its highest good, sick unto death."[1] Doubtless, Shakespeare held the same view, but he knew that love took different forms, that the varieties of love were many, if not infinite. In *A Midsummer Night's Dream* he does not treat all of them but focuses instead on a few major kinds of love: romantic young love, mature love, and married love.

The play opens with an odd combination—or what seems to be a combination—of romantic and mature love. Theseus and Hippolyta are experienced grownups, hardly immature lovers, about to be married; nevertheless, Theseus's opening lines suggest the impatient longing of teenagers. Recognizing that only four days remain until their wedding day, he complains,

> . . . but O, methinks, how slow
> This old moon wanes! She lingers my desires,
> Like to a step-dame or a dowager
> Long withering out a young man's revenue. (1.1.3–6)

The comparison to a young man is apt, although Theseus otherwise hardly fits the description. Hippolyta, by contrast, showing a woman's common sense (typical of Shakespeare's comic heroines), reassures her fiancé that the time will pass quickly enough, as assuredly it does. After recovering a measure of equanimity, Theseus sends his master of revels, Philostrate, to "Stir up the Athenian youth to merriments, / Awake the pert and nimble spirit of mirth" (1.1.12–13) to prepare for the nuptial event. Although not so young himself, he will enjoy the company of young people to entertain him and his bride. Little does he realize what entertainment lies in store.

The interruption by Egeus and three of the young lovers begins part of that entertainment (and ours), though not exactly what Theseus had in mind when he sent off Philostrate. The love between Hermia and Lysander, and Demetrius's interference, abetted by Hermia's father, contrasts with the more settled affection between Theseus and Hippolyta. Egeus, like Brabantio later in *Othello*, is convinced that Lysander has "bewitched" the bosom of his child. Like the old man he is, he cannot understand the true beguilements of young love and believes Lysander has won his daughter's love "With feigning voice verses of feigning love," by which he has "stolen the impression of her fantasy" (1.1.31–32). To him, the love his daughter feels for Lysander is "fantasy," not real, the result of her immaturity, or "unhardened youth" (35). He insists on the prerogative of a parent to determine whom his daughter will marry, and his choice is Demetrius.

On her part, Hermia stands firm on her love for Lysander and refuses to yield to her father's demand. She has the stubbornness of youth, despite the penalties that Theseus reminds her the law retains, should she disobey.[2] Here authority as determined by law,[3] another important theme, comes into direct conflict with love, as it will later on in the relationship between Oberon and Titania. Lysander, too, refuses to yield to Egeus's demand, but, instead of insisting solely on his love, he argues in terms he thinks Egeus will better comprehend:

> I am, my lord, as well-derived as he,
> As well-possessed: my love is more than his,

My fortunes every way as fairly ranked,
If not with vantage, as Demetrius'. (1.1.99–102)

He then offers other arguments that he thinks will enhance his position: unlike Demetrius, he has Hermia's love, and besides, Demetrius is fickle: he has already jilted Helena.

Left alone, Hermia and Lysander commiserate with each other. Lysander reminds his love that "The course of true love never did run smooth" (1.1.134), and he recounts the different kinds of obstacles that have beset lovers in the past. Given the many calamities that may beset them, Hermia sensibly counsels patience (151); to which Lysander replies, "A good persuasion." He immediately hits upon a different plan, however, one that reflects the impetuosity of youth (as it did in *Romeo and Juliet*) : elopement. He has a dowager aunt "Of great revenue" who respects him as her son, and thither he suggests they flee. No sooner does Hermia swear to the plan, than Helena enters with her own love problems.

Forsaken by Demetrius, Helena bemoans the fact and envies Hermia. She asks her friend to teach her how to look "and with what art / You sway the motion of Demetrius' heart" (1.1.192–93). Like the immature young woman she is, she understands little of what truly motivates love. She knows she is as pretty as Hermia; she knows, too, that love is irrational, for in spite of everything, she still loves Demetrius.

Things base and vile, holding no quantity,
Love can transpose to form and dignity.
Love looks not with the eyes, but with the mind,
Therefore is winged Cupid painted blind.
Nor hath love's mind of any judgement taste;
Wings, and no eyes, figure unheedy haste;
And therefore is love said to be a child
Because in choice he is so oft beguiled. (232–39)

Helena is clearly right about the transforming power of love, as subsequent events in the play demonstrate only too vividly. She is right, too, about Cupid's blindness, but, as subsequent events also show, love is often led by the eyes.[4] Shakespeare says as much in the song that precedes Bassanio's casket choice in *The Merchant of Venice*:

> Tell me where is fancy bred,
> Or in the heart or in the head?
> How begot, how nourished?
>   Reply, reply.
> It is engend'red in the eyes,
> With gazing fed, and fancy dies
> In the cradle where it lies. (3.2.63–69)

"Fancy" in this context, of course, refers to love, or perhaps imagined love, not real love. Both Lysander and Demetrius, as well as Titania, will be vigorously led astray by their eyes, once the juice of the flower, appropriately named love-in-idleness, is placed on that part of their anatomy.

After Lysander's eyes have been anointed, he awakes to see Helena before him in the forest, and he immediately professes his love for her. This shows how powerfully irrational love can blind the eyes and pervert the reason. Much of what he says is true, but his point of reference is distorted by the effect of the potion placed on his eyes:

> Who will not change a raven for a dove?
> The will of man is by his reason swayed,
> And reason says you are the worthier maid.
> Things growing are not ripe until their season;
> So I, being young, till now ripe not to reason.
> And touching now the point of human skill,
> Reason becomes the marshall to my will.
> And leads me to your eyes. (2.2.120–27)

In a well-balanced, healthy state, one is controlled by the reason, but it is not reason telling Lysander that Helena is worthier than Hermia. He is, moreover, far from being "ripe," that is, mature, to the point where he is under rational control of his actions.[5] Nor are any of the others during the central episodes in the forest, as they chase each other about, propelled by irrational forces they barely comprehend, if at all.[6] In Ernest Schanzer's interpretation, the love that Helena and Lysander describe "is a love which has no basis in reality, which creates a phantom, a mere shadow of the beloved person; it is a dream. Though it is entirely devoid of judgment the victim is, ironically, under the delusion that he is following reason in his choice."[7]

All this is highly comical, to the audience, though not at all to the lovers themselves. It is also highly erotic. According to Jan Kott, "The

Dream is the most erotic of Shakespeare's plays. In no other tragedy or comedy of his, except *Troilus and Cressida*, is the eroticism expressed so brutally."[8] As evidence for the brutality, he cites, for example, the dialogue at 3.2.260–64, where Lysander yells venom at Hermia, calling her names and desperately trying to throw her off him. In many modern productions, as in Peter Hall's film (see chapter 7), the lovers are often shown scrambling about, their clothes torn and besplattered with mud. Warrant for this description lies partly in Hermia's lines after she battles with Helena and the others and wearily lies down to sleep:

> Never so weary, never so in woe,
>> Bedabbled with dew, and torn with briars—
> I can no further crawl, no further go;
>> My legs can keep no pace with my desires. (3.2.442–45)

According to Kott, the relationship between Titania and Bottom with his ass's head is further evidence of the brutal eroticism in the play. Although Kott overstates the situation, as when he says, "The slender, tender and lyrical Titania longs for animal love" (183), her devotion to the "monster" whom she drags off to bed shows the depths to which irrational love can lead.[9]

When the eyes are restored to their normal function, reason resumes control. Lysander once again loves Hermia, and Titania loathes the sight of the "monster," Bottom (4.1.76). Demetrius's eyes, on the other hand, retain the love potion. He tries as well as he can to explain to the duke what has happened to make him renounce his love for Hermia and return to Helena, but he is wise enough to admit he really does not know the reason:

> . . . good my lord, I wot not by what power
> (But by some power it is), my love to Hermia
> Melted as the snow, seems to me now
> As the remembrance of an idle gaud
> Which in my childhood I did dote upon;
> And all the faith, the virtue of my heart,
> The object and pleasure of mine eye,
> Is only Helena. To her, my lord,
> Was I betrothed ere I saw Hermia;
> But like a sickness did I loathe this food.
> But, as in health come to my natural taste,

> Now do I wish it, love it, long for it,
> And will for evermore be true to it. (4.1.161–73)

The love potion that Oberon has directed Puck to administer thus has another function. Not only can it cause someone to fall in love, but (guided by a benevolent power) it can restore a true love that under some other, less benign influence has been misdirected.

Love may and often does lead to marriage, as it does for these young couples and for Theseus and Hippolyta. For Theseus and Hippolyta, reason and love have joined together and are no longer in opposition, despite an inauspicious beginning (1.1.16–17).[10] Oberon and Titania's marriage, however, runs into serious trouble when they quarrel over the little Indian boy, offspring of Titania's devotee who died in childbirth. She refuses to turn him over to her husband, and as a result the world of nature has turned topsy-turvy. Their quarrel is largely though not entirely a matter of "who's boss"; that is, male supremacy versus female rights.[11] In Shakespeare's patriarchal world, there was no question about it: the husband ruled.[12] Oberon feels he has to teach Titania a lesson, and feeling entirely within his rights, he resorts to a rather vile trick to do so.

Although she speaks a good deal of romantic love poetry to him, Titania's adoration of Bottom is not so much romantic love as it is a function of the love-madness that characterizes the young couples' plight in the forest scenes. "Here, in the infatuation of the Queen of fairies for a weaver metamorphosed into an ass," Schanzer states, "we have displayed the full absurdity of the kind of love which is engendered in the imagination only, uncorrected by judgment and the senses" (28). This is not quite accurate, however, for Titania's eyes are not exactly blinded; her eyesight is distorted by the powerful influence of love-in-idleness, which has led her to view Bottom as a handsome as well as a wise man worthy of her adoration. If we can take Theseus's word for it, she is not entirely unaware of what is happening: when he recently met her in the forest gathering flowers with which to bedeck Bottom's temples, he tells Puck (4.1.43–60), he upbraided her and fell out with her so that she began to weep and beg him to stop. As soon as Oberon finished taunting her, she relented and straightaway agreed to give him the Indian boy.

In this manner Oberon resumes full control as Titania's lord and master. He applies the antidote to her eyes, shows her the grotesque image she adored, and wins her love and devotion once more. Her words when she awakens convey immediately her obeisance and her horror at what she has experienced:

> My Oberon, what visions have I seen!
> Methought I was enamoured of an ass. (4.1.73–74)

Calling for music and taking Titania's hand, Oberon begins their dance of newfound amity. Appropriately, he promises to dance "tomorrow midnight solemnly" at Duke Theseus's house "triumphantly / And bless it to all fair prosperity" (83–86). It is a triumph for him and for reason over passion, or willfulness, and the end of love-madness for everyone.

THE ART OF PERFORMANCE

According to a number of critics and theater directors, the play-within-the-play, "Pyramus and Thisbe," for all its unintentional farce as performed by the rude mechanicals, is at the heart of *A Midsummer Night's Dream.*

> As an actor, dramatist, and "sharer" in the finances of a theatre company, Shakespeare was deeply concerned with the ways in which actors and audience accept the "truth" of dramatic illusion, and, as a poet, he saw in these relationships an image of man's recognition of imagined truths. So the significance of the play-within-the-play in *A Midsummer Night's Dream* is enforced by the use of the same device in other comedies and in history-plays and tragedies.[13]

Similarly, as he began rehearsals of his epoch-making production of the *Dream*, Peter Brook announced that the play-within-the-play was the "key" to everything. For Brook, it was a microcosm of the play as a whole, raising fundamental questions of the nature of reality and the nature of acting.[14] To some of these questions we now turn.

At their very first meeting, Quince and his fellow thespians ponder the implications of what they are about to undertake. When Quince informs Bottom what part he is to play in their "interlude" before the duke and his duchess, Bottom inquires what kind of role Pyramus is—a lover or a tyrant (1.2.17). Told that he is "A lover that kills himself, most gallant, for love," Bottom responds, "That will ask some tears in the true performing of it. If I do it, let the audience look to their eyes: I will move storms, I will condole, in some measure" (18–21). Bottom is already aware of audience reaction and the necessity for "true" enactment of a role. Quince seconds his concern for the effect on an audience a few minutes later when Bottom offers to perform the role of lion also, bragging about how well he can roar (57–59). Quince worries, "And you should do it too terribly, you would fright the Duchess and the ladies that they would shriek; and that were enough to hang us all." To this Bottom responds that he "will roar you as gently as any sucking dove. I will roar you and 'twere any nightingale" (60–67).

Quince insists that Bottom play only Pyramus, to which he reluctantly agrees. The issue Shakespeare wanted to raise in all this, it seems, is the relation between illusion and reality and both the actors' understanding of it and the audience's. The issue gathers momentum in the mechanicals' next scene, when they are in the forest and beginning their rehearsals. Bottom questions the advisability of Pyramus's killing himself on stage with his sword, which, he feels, "the ladies cannot abide" (3.1.10). Snout agrees that it is "a parlous fear!" and when Starveling suggests that the killing must be omitted, Bottom proposes a "device" to make all well: Peter Quince will write a prologue reassuring the audience that the actors will really do no harm with their swords. Furthermore, he says that the prologue must inform the audience that he, Pyramus, is not really Pyramus, but Bottom the weaver, and by this means put the audience out of fear (3.1.11–17).

The trepidation of the troupe is thus allayed, at least for the moment, until other questions are raised about the lion, about bringing moonlight into the chamber, and about the wall. That Quince does not, in fact, deliver the prologue Bottom proposes is irrelevant here. More to the point is that, during the actual performance before Theseus and his court, the various actors—and especially Bottom as Pyramus—come out of their roles at different moments to explain who they are, what they are doing, and why. For they have not fully understood, if at all, the nature of dramatic illusion, even though, as Bottom seems to know, that to get the right effect from the audience, a part must be played "truly." Their confusion, however, coupled with the stage audience's remarks, enables the theater audience to make the proper connection.[15]

When Snout, for example, enters as Wall and gives his speech explaining who he is and why he is costumed as he is—"This loam, this rough-cast, and this stone doth show / That I am that same wall; the truth is so" (5.1.159–60)—Theseus turns to Demetrius and asks, "Would you desire lime and hair to speak better?" To which Demetrius replies,

"It is the wittiest partition that ever I heard discourse, my lord" (163–65). Their comments highlight for the theater audience not only how amateurish the performance is that they are witnessing, but how naive or innocent the actors are in what they are about.[16] Simultaneously, Theseus and Demetrius are surrogates for the theater audience who, in identifying with them, for a moment become part of the reality of the play that Shakespeare is presenting.

Comments from the stage audience continue throughout the performance of "Pyramus and Thisbe." Among the more important ones are those imbedded in the following dialogue between Hippolyta and Theseus:

> *Hippolyta* This is the silliest stuff that ever I heard.
>
> *Theseus* The best in this kind are but shadows; and the worst are no worse, if imagination amend them.
>
> *Hippolyta* It must be your imagination then, and not theirs.
>
> *Theseus* If we imagine no worse of them than they of themselves, they may pass for excellent men. (5.1.204–9)

This appeal to the audience's imagination lies at the heart of any dramatic performance, for a successful stage presentation depends, as one critic has maintained, upon the imaginative cooperation of playwright, producers, and audience.[17] Without a "willing suspension of disbelief," we cannot fully enjoy the performance of a play. At the same time, paradoxically, as Dr. Samuel Johnson reminds us, we remain aware that we are in a theater and not in Athens, Rome, or London. This is another function of "multiconsciousness" evoked by Shakespeare's *Dream*.

REALITY AND ILLUSION

If the art of performance depends on illusion—and illusion that for a while we accept as real—much else in *A Midsummer Night's Dream* also develops the basic opposition between reality and appearance.[18] Love, as we have seen, becomes problematical when reality and illusion become confused. At night in the forest—and night, like sleep and shadows, fosters illusion[19]—Lysander, believing he loves Helena, rejects Hermia, but he is under an illusion induced by the magic potion derived from love-in-idleness. Demetrius believes he loves Hermia and despises Helena; but however real his emotions seem at the beginning of the play, the same magic induces him to reconsider his position, and he eventually learns the reality of his abiding love for Helena.[20] Similarly, Theseus's battle against the Amazons, with Hippolyta as their leader, must have seemed the result of real enough provocation. In conquest, however, the attitude toward his captive queen changes, and he recognizes a new reality—his love for Hippolyta and his wish to wed her "in another key" (1.1.16–19).

Like Lysander's doting upon Helena in the central scenes of the play, Titania's doting upon Bottom—monstrous as he appears with his ass's head—is the effect of a magically induced illusion. After Oberon applies the antidote to her eyes, she sees the illusion for what it was, however real it may have seemed to her at the time of her infatuation. This of course is the crux of the situation: how can anyone distinguish the apparent reality—the illusion—from the true reality?

Shakespeare provided a clue, ironically, in Lysander's lines (quoted earlier) when he awakens and sees Helena:

> The will of man is by his reason swayed,
> And reason says you are the worthier maid. (2.2.122–23)

Lysander is correct: under normal conditions, a person's will, or desire, is properly directed by reason. When passion or emotion takes control, the will becomes misdirected. This is good Tudor psychology, deriving from Platonic philosophy. Accordingly, Hamlet upbraids his mother in the Closet Scene, arguing that she has allowed reason to pander to her will; that is, she has permitted her reason to become subverted and hence subordinated to the dictates of her lust.[21] Lysander believes he is acting reasonably, unaware that he is under the influence of love-in-idleness, which has distorted his reason, if not also his vision.

If one cannot depend on reason, what then? One recourse is to authority which, under the best of circumstances, is directed by right reason. Hence, Egeus appeals to authority in the person of Duke Theseus when his daughter will not listen to reason as he presents it to her. Egeus is convinced that Hermia is under the influence of illusion-producing agents, such as "rhymes," "love-tokens," and other gifts that Lysander has used to woo her (1.1.27–38). Appeals to Egeus's better reason made by Lysander (99–105) as well as by Hermia (50–56) fall on deaf ears. Although Shakespeare did not significantly distinguish one suitor from the other, if at all, Egeus is under the illusion that Demetrius is the better man. For the moment, authority sides with Egeus, though only on the

Bas relief (Bottom and Titania) from the Folger Shakespeare Library exterior facade. By permission of the Folger Shakespeare Library.

basis of a father's right, in law, to determine whom his child shall marry. Theseus therefore warns Hermia of the consequences if she does not obey her father's wishes. Authority later demonstrates a superior reason, when Theseus discovers the lovers in the forest so sweetly and correctly coupled with each other. The duke, allowing superior reason to supersede law, now decides to "overbear" Egeus's "will." The couples may marry whom they have chosen, and they are invited to join Theseus and Hippolyta at the temple for a triple wedding ceremony (4.1.176–82).

What has caused this "gentle concord in the world" (4.1.140) to come about is partly the return of right reason to the lovers. That, of course, is not the whole story; Oberon's role has also been important. Of this the young people are very imperfectly aware. Demetrius recognizes that "some power" has been involved in straightening things out for them, though he does not know what power it is. We, the audience, do. Is the fairy king merely an illusion? Is there a providence that directs our destiny, as (to cite *Hamlet* again) the Prince of Denmark asserts?[22]

Shakespeare, indirectly in this play, through Oberon's interventions, suggests an answer. Otherwise, and wisely too, he lets Bottom comment on his own experience:

> I have had a most rare vision. I had a dream, past the wit of man to say what dream it was. Man is but an ass if he go about to expound this dream. Methought I was—there is no man can tell what. Methought I was—and methought I had—but man is but a patched fool if he will offer to say what methought I had. The eye of man hath not heard, the ear of man hath not seen, man's hand is not able to taste, his tongue to conceive, nor his heart to report what my dream was! (4.1.200–207)

Bottom's monologue is a garbled reference to 1 Cor. 2.9–10, but as R. A. Foakes's note claims, it has more point than Bottom realizes. Foakes therefore quotes the relevant scriptural passage:

> The eye of man hath not seene, and the eare hath not heard, neither have entered into the heart of man, the things which God hath prepared for them that love him. But God hath revealed them unto us by his spirit; for the spirit searcheth all things, yea the deepe things of God![23]

As the passage he paraphrases indicates, Bottom's dream, or vision, "hath no bottom"; it is fathomless. But also like the matter to which the scripture refers, it is real and not an illusion, though not sensible or comprehensible to human intelligence by reason alone.[24]

FRIENDSHIP

A minor theme in *A Midsummer Night's Dream* is the theme of friendship. The friendship between women, as between Hermia and Helena, is more pronounced in this play than that between men. In the first scene, for example, the friendship between the two young women is indicated by Hermia's compassion for Helena and her willingness to confide in her. Although Helena's sorrow derives from her erstwhile lover's fickleness and his suit to obtain her best friend in marriage instead of her,

Helena does not reveal any bitter resentment toward Hermia, merely self-disparaging regret (1.1.181–201). As testimony to their strong friendship, Hermia reveals that she and Lysander plan to elope and even tells her where they plan to meet in the forest. Helena's betrayal of the plan to Demetrius is prompted more by a desire to win a modicum of favor from him than by a sense that she is betraying her friend. As she says,

> for this intelligence,
> If I have thanks it is a dear expense;
> But herein mean I to enrich my pain,
> To have his sight thither, and back again. (248–51)

None of the commentators gloss "a dear expense" as referring to the sacrifice of her friendship with Hermia, though this in fact is what eventually occurs, if temporarily, as a result of her betrayal. Critics tend, rather, to interpret the phrase as a reference to what it will cost Helena in Demetrius's love by enabling him to pursue Hermia.[25]

The extent of the sacrifice of friendship Helena unwittingly makes becomes explicit during the contretemps between her and Hermia in the forest. At first, Helena is astonished when Hermia appears and Lysander rejects her. She believes her friend is part of the conspiracy—the cruel joke they are playing on her—and in her complaint she appeals to the long friendship she and Hermia have shared:

> Injurious Hermia, most ungrateful maid,
> Have you conspired, have you with these contrived
> To bait me with this foul derision?
> Is all the counsel we two have shared,
> The sisters' vows, the hours that we have spent
> When we have chid the hasty-footed time
> For parting us—O, is all forgot?
> All schooldays' friendship, childhood innocence?
> We, Hermia, like two artificial gods
> Have with our needles created both one flower,
> Both on one sampler, sitting on one cushion,
> Both warbling of one song, both in one key,
> As if our hands, our sides, voices, and minds
> Had been incorporate. So we grew together
> Like to a double cherry, seeming parted,
> But yet an union in partition,
> Two lovely berries moulded on one stem. (3.2.195–211)

No finer description of, or tribute to, a "sisterhood" between two young women has anyone ever written.[26] The repetition of two as one, beginning at line 203, continues throughout the passage, emphasizing the closeness of the two friends; it reaches a climax in the image of the "double cherry, seeming parted" growing together. Helena's sense of betrayal is thus all the more acute when she thinks Hermia has joined with the men to rend their love asunder and scorn her. She has no sense whatever that it is her betrayal of Hermia's confidence earlier which has led to this state of affairs. On the contrary, she mistakenly believes she is the one betrayed in friendship, that everything has been a plot to humiliate and degrade her.

The ideal friendship between two women, here so well defined even as it is about to dissolve momentarily, Shakespeare presented elsewhere, in the devotion of the two cousins, Celia and Rosalind, in *As You Like It*. When Celia's father, the usurping Duke Frederick, banishes Rosalind, Celia vigorously objects, defending her and claiming the closest possible identity with her.

> If she be traitor,
> Why, so am I. We still have slept together,
> Rose at an instant, learn'd, play'd, eat together,
> And whereso'er we went, like Juno's swans,
> Still we went coupled and inseparable. (1.3.72–76)

Frederick is adamant, and so is Celia. When her father refuses to relent, she says that she cannot live out of her cousin's company (86), and she proves she means it by following Rosalind into exile in the Forest of Arden.

Hermia's response to Helena's passionate words, however, is simply one of amazement. She does not scorn her, she says, but "it seems that you scorn me" (3.2.221). She is thoroughly confused, and so is Helena, though she does not realize it. Only when the men resume their protestations of love for Helena, challenging each other to a fight (245–55), and Lysander renounces his former love, demeaning Hermia and wishing her gone (257 ff.), does the situation completely deteriorate. In the process, the friendship between Helena and Hermia also deteriorates; they fall to name-calling and physical threats (282 ff.), until Helena, frightened, runs away (340–43).

As soon as Puck restores each to their proper love, and Theseus overrides Egeus's demands, the friendship is restored. As the couples contemplate their experience, the women have very little to say, but what they say is significant:

> *Hermia* Methinks I see these things with parted eye,
> When everything seems double.
> *Helena*   So methinks;
> And I have found Demetrius, like a jewel,
> Mine own, and not mine own. (4.1.186–89)

They are not quite sure what has happened to them—everything seems ambiguous, or "double"—but the animosity that flared up between them is clearly over. They do not have much else to say for the rest of the play—nothing, in fact, in all of act 5 where, like good wives, they let their husbands do the talking. The amity, if silently, is revived.[27]

Male friendships are also developed in *A Midsummer Night's Dream*, although at a lower level of society. Without question, the workmen whom Peter Quince assembles in 1.2 know and like each other. The clearest evidence of this camaraderie appears in 4.2, where the men sit around and mourn the loss of their friend Bottom. Starveling is sure he has been "transported";[28] the others speak highly of his thespian ability and his wit. Thus they are overjoyed when he reappears as himself, that is, without his ass's head, and he calls out, "Where are these lads? Where are these hearts?" (20). Their reunion further evidences their friendship and solidarity. In all the excitement over his return, Bottom promises that he will "discourse wonders," but immediately afterwards he swears not to say anything. He is not being coy or cruel, just being Bottom, delivering the news that their play is preferred and they had better get ready to perform.

From ancient times through the Renaissance, friendship between men was regarded as the highest form of social relationship, even surpassing that between man and woman in matrimony.[29] While Shakespeare did not develop or suggest the ideal of masculine friendship here as he does, say, in *The Merchant of Venice* regarding Antonio's relationship with Bassanio—men of a much higher social class than the rude mechanicals in *Dream*—we can infer something of the warm bonds of friendship that connect these men. Oberon's relationship with Puck is of a different order entirely—hardly one of friendship but more that of master and servant. Nor can much be said of the other male relationships, such as that of Egeus and Theseus. If friendship is not a primary theme, at least among men, in *A Midsummer Night's Dream*, it does have its place in the relationship between women.[30]

HARMONY FROM DISCORD

It is axiomatic that tragedy moves from well-being to catastrophe, whereas comedy moves in the opposite direction, from difficulty to a happy resolution of that difficulty. Not all of Shakespeare's comedies fit neatly into the comic paradigm thus described. In *Love's Labor's Lost*, for example, Jack does not end up with his Jill but has to undergo a period of penitence and education before that possible eventuality. On the other hand, in *The Comedy of Errors* and *Two Gentlemen of Verona* the confusions and disruptions are satisfactorily resolved, at least where the major characters are concerned, as far as Shakespeare allows us to enter into their milieu.[31] In *A Midsummer Night's Dream*, finding "the concord of this discord" (5.1.60) becomes the subject not only of Theseus's question regarding the "very tragical mirth" that Quince & Co. want to stage, but also of every aspect of the play's dramatic structure.

Although the *Dream* begins, rather than ends, with the peaceful resolution of warfare between Theseus and Hippolyta, culminating in their wedding plans, such harmony is immediately broken, as noted, by Egeus's interruption. His complaint against his daughter's insubordination introduces one of the major themes of discord, followed shortly afterwards by the discord between Oberon and Titania. The latter has involved discord throughout the worlds of nature and human activity, resulting in an upheaval in the seasons, the weather, and the pursuit of both work and pleasure among mortal beings (2.1.82–116). We have seen by what means these conflicts are resolved. Oberon's intercession leads to the proper coupling of the four young lovers, and the harsh lesson he teaches Titania brings about her ultimate acquiescence to his demands and their subsequent reconciliation. The dialogue between Theseus and Hippolyta in 4.1 about the "music" of his Spartan hounds (4.1.103–24) is by way of commenting indirectly upon the fairy couple's newfound harmony and introducing the concord now of the young couples.

What Hippolyta describes as "So musical a discord, such sweet thunder" (4.1.115), referring to the baying of the hounds as she went hunting once with Hercules and Cadmus, epitomizes the action of *A Midsummer Night's Dream*.[32] This is reason, again, for including the dialogue just before she and Theseus come upon the sleeping lovers and just after the awakening of Titania. Later, Theseus indicates to her how best to reconcile themselves to the woefully amateurish performance of the workmen as they put on their interlude of "Pyramus and Thisbe" (5.1.205–9). The farcical presentation of the tragedy is Shakespeare's answer to Theseus's question on how to find "the concord of this discord," that is the oxymoron posed by "tragical mirth" (5.1.57).

At the end, Oberon, Titania, and their train join together to bless all the newlyweds, promising them constant love and healthy progeny:

> So shall all the couples three
> Ever true in loving be,
> And the blots of nature's hand
> Shall not in their issue stand. (5.1.385–88)

Finally, turning to the theater audience, Puck pleads for a concord between them and the actors and offers a solution for any offense that the cast may have committed: the audience may simply imagine that "this weak and idle theme," their performance, was simply a dream they experienced while they slumbered there (401–6). He promises that, if granted pardon, the actors will do better next time, and he concludes by asking for conciliatory applause, not hisses (the "serpent's tongue"):

> So, good night unto you all.
> Give me your hands, if we be friends,
> And Robin shall restore amends. (5.1.414–16)

NOTES

1. Saul Bellow, *Ravelstein*. New York: Viking Press, 2000, 15.

2. Compare Alexander Leggatt, *Shakespeare's Comedy of Love*. London: Methuen, 1974, 92. Against her father's attack, Hermia's inarticulate defense "suggests that love is a force bearing down all normal authority. . . . It gives Hermia the courage to defy her father and the Duke in open court, and to accept the pains and trials love must always bear."

3. On the Elizabethan legal context, see chapter 2 in this volume.

4. Ralph Berry, *Shakespeare's Comedies*. Princeton, N.J.: Princeton University Press, 1972, 91: "Reason stands by cool judgment; love, by pure subjectivity, for the 'eye' in this comedy is a channel of passion as well as an organ of perception."

5. Compare R. W. Dent, "Imagination in *A Midsummer Night's Dream*,"

Shakespeare Quarterly 15 (1964), 115–29; reprinted in *"A Midsummer Night's Dream": Critical Essays*, ed. Dorothea Kehler, 85–102. New York: Garland, 1998. References are to the reprint. "[W]hen Lysander eventually boasts of his use of reason in preferring a dove to a raven his argument . . . is indeed rational. Our laughter stems from recognizing that it is so only accidentally, as rationalization" (86).

6. The following dialogue between Titania and Bottom, when she is awakened by his singing, further brings out the opposition of reason to love as well as the influence of eyesight:

> *Titania* I pray thee, gentle mortal, sing again;
> Mine ear is much enamoured of thy note.
> So is mine eye enthrallèd to thy shape,
> And thy fair virtue's force perforce doth move me
> On the first view to say, to swear, I love thee.
>
> *Bottom* Methinks, mistress, you should have little reason for that. And yet, to say the truth, reason and love keep little company together nowadays; the more the pity that some honest neighbours will not make them friends. (3.1.114–22)

7. Ernest Schanzer, "*A Midsummer Night's Dream*," in *Shakespeare: The Comedies*, ed. Kenneth Muir, 28. Englewood Cliffs, N.J.: Prentice-Hall, 1965.

8. Jan Kott, *Shakespeare Our Contemporary*, trans. Boleslaw Taborski. 2d ed. London: Methuen, 1967, 175. Compare Thomas McFarland, *Shakespeare's Pastoral Comedy*. Chapel Hill: University of North Carolina Press, 1972. He argues against this view on the basis of the play's tone. For him the play's eroticism is only "a barely perceptible undercurrent, a kind of elegant hint of other things" (80).

9. Kott goes much too far later in this passage when he declares that "This is the lover she wanted and dreamed of; only she never wanted to admit it, even to herself. Sleep frees her from inhibitions. The monstrous ass is being raped by the poetic Titania, while she keeps on chattering about flowers" (*Shakespeare Our Contemporary*, 183). Kott's views have led a number of modern directors to present Titania and Bottom engaging in intercourse.

10. See Schanzer, "*Midsummer Night's Dream*," 29.

11. More subtly, the controversy also concerns Oberon's desire to take the boy, who has now grown to a suitable age, out of the company of women and into his own train. See Tom Clayton, " 'So Bright Things Come to Confusion'; or, What Else Is *A Midsummer Night's Dream About?*" in *Shakespeare: Text and Theater: Essays in Honor of Jay L. Halio*, ed. Lois Potter and Arthur F. Kinney, 71–73. Newark: University of Delaware Press, 1999. Clayton redirects critical concern toward the *boy's* interest and argues that "in the patriarchal fairy culture, *his* interests are best served by his joining Oberon" (71). Compare Gail Kern Paster and Skiles Howard, *"A Midsummer Night's Dream": Texts and*

Contexts. Boston: Bedford/St. Martin's, 1999, 166: "One of patriarchy's major tasks was to take the young boy from the tender care of women and to inculcate in him the repressive self-control and desire for mastery that he would need in order to take up the obligations of his adult station."

12. For orthodox Elizabethan views, see, for example, Edwin Sandys, "Sermon 16," in *Sermons* (London, 1585), 319–21.

13. John Russell Brown, *Shakespeare and His Comedies*. 2d ed. London: Methuen, 1962, 91.

14. Jay L. Halio, *Shakespeare in Performance: A Midsummer Night's Dream*. Manchester, England: Manchester University Press, 1994, 54. See also David Selbourne, *The Making of "A Midsummer Night's Dream."* London: Methuen, 1982.

15. Compare Dent, "Imagination," 97–98:

> What the mechanicals fail to understand, obviously, is the audience's awareness that drama is drama, to be viewed imaginatively but not mistaken, in any realistic sense, for reality. . . . On the one hand they fear their audience will imagine what it sees is real, mistaking "shadows" for reality; on the other, they think the audience unable to imagine what they cannot see.

16. Compare C. L. Barber, *Shakespeare's Festive Comedy*. Princeton, N.J.: Princeton University Press, 1959: "What the clowns forget . . . is that a killing of a lion in a play, however plausibly presented, is a mental event. Because, like children, they do not discriminate between imaginary and real events, they are literal about fiction" (150–51).

17. Dent, "Imagination," 100. Compare Stanley Wells's comment in the Introduction to his New Penguin edition of the play (Harmondsworth, England: Penguin Books, 1967):

> The actors of the interlude need the imaginative participation of their stage-audience if they are to succeed. This is as true of the play itself as of the play within the play. It is all unreal; yet, if we too bring our imaginations to it, it may grow to something of great constancy, a universal harmony, a music of the spheres in which each sings its own song. (36)

18. Another way to approach this theme is to consider the opposition between night and day, dream and waking. See Leggatt, *Shakespeare's Comedy of Love*, 105–9.

19. Compare Berry, *Shakespeare's Comedies*, 94, who cites Anne Righter's *Shakespeare and the Idea of the Play*: "night, sleep, shadows, and dreams are all symbols of illusion."

20. See Clayton, "So Bright Things Come to Confusion," who argues that Demetrius's situation "seems a case of homeopathic medicine, in effect a cure of the infection of doting on Hermia's eyes" (73).

21. *Hamlet*, 3.4.85–88 (but see the entire passage beginning at line 39).

22. Ibid., 5.1.10–11, 219–24.

23. In the note in his New Cambridge Shakespeare edition, R. A. Foakes (Cambridge, England: Cambridge University Press, 1984) cites the Bishops' Bible, which is closer to Bottom's version than the Geneva Bible and therefore probably the one that Shakespeare parodies here. The wider context of the chapter is also worth comparing.

24. On the significance of the entire scene, compare Berry, *Shakespeare's Comedies*, 99: "The 'awakening' sequence, perhaps the most poignant moment of poetry in the play, is in theatrical terms presented as a return to daylight and sanity."

25. See, for example, Peter Holland's note (*A Midsummer Night's Dream*, Oxford: Oxford University Press, 1994) and compare Harold Brooks's note in *A Midsummer Night's Dream*, London: Methuen, 1979.

26. Compare René Girard, *A Theater of Envy: William Shakespeare*. New York: Oxford University Press, 1991, 33–34: "Hermia and Helena are the same type of friends as Valentine and Proteus [in *The Two Gentlemen of Verona*]: they have lived together since infancy; they have been educated together; they always act, think, feel, and desire alike."

27. In *Women and the English Renaissance* (Urbana: University of Illinois Press, 1984), Linda Woodbridge comments on "the most enviable facet of female friendship," which she says was "the warmth and spontaneity of the emotional support women seemed able to give each other in times of crisis," which contrasts with male friendships that "merely crumble during a crisis" (239). While this is true of the Celia-Rosalind relationship, the friendship obviously breaks down in the *Dream*, although under quite different circumstances. If a friendship between Lysander and Demetrius ever existed, it is not so indicated (though it might be inferred) in the play.

28. His meaning is unclear. He could mean "carried away to some other realm," as Foakes (*Midsummer Night's Dream*) suggests in his gloss, although it might also be Starveling's error for "translated," which Quince had used earlier (3.1.98).

29. See, for example, Sir Thomas Elyot, *The Booke of the Governour* (1531), Book II, chapter 11; Edmund Spenser, *The Faerie Queene* (1596), Book IV, 9:1–3; and Michel de Montaigne, "Of Friendship" (c. 1580), in *The Complete Works of Montaigne*, trans. Donald Frame (Stanford: Stanford University Press, 1957), 135–44.

30. Hippolyta does not have any female friendships in this play, although in some modern productions she is shown as highly sympathtic to Hermia in 1.1 and forming a subtle but sure solidarity with her and Helena later on. It is she, after all, more than Theseus who is willing to accept the couples' account of their experience in the forest as more than mere imagination but rather "something of great constancy" (5.1.23–27). Titania is also without female friendship, having only her subservient fairies to attend on her.

31. Critics take a different view of the ending of *Two Gentlemen of Verona*.

According to Berry in *Shakespeare's Comedies*, "[T]he magnanimous/fatuous/ ungentlemanly action of Valentine in disposing of Silvia . . . has excited the horror of critics on moral or aesthetic grounds" (50).

32. Compare Harold C. Goddard, *The Meaning of Shakespeare*. Chicago: University of Chicago Press, 1951. According to Goddard, the whole passage "is as nearly a perfect metaphor as could be conceived for *A Midsummer Night's Dream* itself and for the incomparable counterpoint with which its own confusions and discords are melted into the 'sweet thunder' of a single musical effect" (75).

5

CRITICAL APPROACHES

Many varied critical approaches, including those apparent in the fore-going chapters, may assist in viewing and more fully understanding the bountiful riches of *A Midsummer Night's Dream*. Among these other approaches are psychoanalytical criticism; feminist (or gender) criticism; analysis through New Historicism and Cultural Materialism; myth, ritual, and folklore studies; and the play in performance, both on stage and on screen. The last approach is the subject of chapters 6 and 7 of this book, as the play has a long and important stage history. In this chapter, less familiar but nonetheless significant alternative approaches are considered.

PSYCHOANALYTICAL CRITICISM

Psychoanalytical criticism of Shakespeare's plays properly begins with Sigmund Freud, the founder of psychoanalysis, and his principal follow-ers, including C. G. Jung, whose approach is rather different. Although Freud did not write an essay on *A Midsummer Night's Dream*, as he did on *The Merchant of Venice* and *King Lear*, he made several comments that demonstrate a psychoanalytical approach to the play. Norman Hol-land recorded a number of those comments. For example, Freud did not hold much stock in the fairies, but he found significance in Titania's actions.

> In the neuroses belief is transposed; it is withheld from the *repressed* material if it forces its way to reproduction [consciousness?] and—as a punishment, one might say—is transposed on to the *defensive* ma-

terial. So Titania, who refused to love her rightful husband Oberon, was obliged instead to shower her love upon Bottom, the ass of her imagination.[1]

Holland also recorded additional comments reported by Theodore Reik. One of them comes from an unpublished lecture delivered in Vienna, where Freud suggested that the play was concerned with "the maliciousness of objects," a particular case of the magical, animistic thinking of children and primitives.[2] Freud had a high opinion of Theseus's description of the creative imagination, and a disciple of his, Josef Breuer, applied Theseus's description of the play-within-the-play ("The best of this kind are but shadows") to physiological explanations of the psychic processes.[3]

Holland cites a later follower of Freud, Jack Lindsay, who claims that, by making the fairies miniscule in size, Shakespeare returned the fairies' sexuality from the immorality of adult-sized beings to "a pure and satisfying contact with the mother." This temporary regression, moreover, according to Lindsay, allowed Shakespeare to free himself from his fear and enslavement to his own mother. The end of the play thus liberates the energies of love, as it does again later in *The Tempest*.[4] Weston A. Gui's analysis empasizes the dream motif in the play. He regards Bottom's as the key dream, since he is the only one who sees and resides with the fairies: he lives his dream—a dream that, according to Gui, is very motherly. He is fed, fondled, and in every way nurtured. Since his dream "hath no bottom," Gui interprets this as meaning that Bottom is reliving childhood blissfulness, without any responsibilities for cleanliness. His transformation partly into an animal symbolizes the transformation of humanity into animality in the sexual act.[5]

Donald F. Jacobson interprets the play in terms of the psychology of feminine development. Titania's theft of the little Indian prince corresponds, he says, to the fantasy of young girls' stealing a baby from their mothers. From the little boy's point of view, the issue is one of sexual identification. Will he become one of Oberon's knights, or remain bedecked with flowers in Titania's train? Even more significant for feminine development are the episodes involving the four human lovers. Jacobson believes that Demetrius represents Hermia's father, while Helena, who is tall, represents a mother figure. Hermia breaks away from both when she finds a male, non-incestuous lover in Lysander. The ending of the play involves surrendering oedipal wishes, as Demetrius (the father) can then marry Helena (the mother), with no objection from Hermia (the daughter). Jacobson's point is that *A Midsummer Night's Dream* demonstrates how a woman must give up oedipal wishes in order to mature.[6]

Holland agrees with Morton Kaplan[7] that both of the preceding readings of the play are "grossly overstated" and simplistic, although he has argued that they pave the way for psychoanalytical interpretations. Holland accepts the argument that the play deals with oedipal themes: "winning a man or woman tabooed by the king-father through transforming either oneself or what one loves or the parental environment."[8] The adaptive mechanism the play offers, he says, is a regression to a wood of childhood imaginings where self and object are not clearly differentiated, there to effect "appropriate transformations."

Taking a Jungian approach to *A Midsummer Night's Dream*, Alex Aronson interprets the forest which the young lovers enter as regressive darkness. The first sentence sets up his argument, from which everything else follows: "The path that leads across the forest to the temple takes man out of the dark labyrinth of his unconscious toward the light of consciousness, from the confusion of uncontrolled affects to the daylight solemnity of the marriage ritual." The lovers' meeting place is "the still and whirling point of the unconscious, the maternal womb where they are translated into sleep, and dreams create images of life and death, reflecting the confusion of a disordered libido."[9] Puck becomes an instrument of the unconscious, an archetypal figure, a representative of the "Trickster-figure" that Jung discovered in Native American mythology. Accordingly, he is "God, man, and animal at once," both subhuman and superman, bestial and divine, whose chief characteristic is his unconsciousness. Despite his phallic qualities, his sex is optional.[10] Whereas conventional literary theory views Puck from the outside, this approach sees him as part of the lovers' unconscious risen to the surface.[11]

Aronson's analysis includes many such Jungian interpretations. It is especially perceptive in helping to understand the symbolism of the forest and the events that take place there. For example, after quoting at length Jung's symbolic rendering of a forest (206), Aronson asserts that when the lovers enter the wood, "they become, as it were, prisoners of a collective dream, a manifestation of their own unconscious. This particular kind of dream is the more readily available as their libido has been driven back upon itself and now looks for shelter 'among the trees' " (207). The archetypal tree, as it appears in myths and dreams, is "a symbol of the libido whose object at one time was the mother" (207). Much of Aronson's Jungian analysis follows from these interpretations, as in his discussion of the relationship between Titania and Bottom: "The symbolic sexual act performed between tree and ass constitutes a kind of primitive equation guaranteeing renewal on earth" (210).

In an essay using Hermia's dream as a basis, Holland recapitulated what he calls the three phases of psychoanalytical approaches to literature.

> The first is typical of the first phase of psychoanalysis: we would use Hermia's dream as an illustration of someone's unconscious made conscious. In the second phase, we would place her dream within a system of ego functions. Finally—today—we would use this airy nothing to symbolize ourselves to ourselves.[12]

Holland begins examining Hermia's dream in light of the first phase. The serpent in her dream signifies, in Freudian terms, a penis or phallus, which is split between the attacking serpent and her lover, Lysander, smiling at a distance. Borrowing a topic from Eric Erikson, Holland sees in this dream something fundamental to Hermia's character. He returns to the speeches in her first scene, wherein he detects a recurring pattern, "a concern for alternatives, for other possibilities, or for an elsewhere"— some alternative, that is, that would help amend something closer to herself (3). By contrast, Helena tries to cope with her problems by establishing a contradiction or opposition and then by trying to become that opposite (19, n. 5).

Hermia's dream thus dramatizes her "parted eye," which she describes after being awakened by Theseus, in all its divisions: "in the double telling, in the here and there of Lysander and the serpent, and in the very content of the dream—her effort to save herself by getting the serpent away and bringing Lysander closer" (Holland 1980, 3–4). Holland believes that by tracing the various levels of the adolescent girl's development—oedipal, phallic, and oral—through the dream, the same theme of amendment can be shown (4). Following the symbols and libidinal levels of her dream would be the classical way of analyzing it, grounding the analysis on the free associations of the dreamer. But since this is a literary text and not an actual dreamer, the associations do not "float up from the couch." The analyst can only infer Hermia's associations, which Holland then proceeds to do. He concluded that the sexual symbolism of Hermia's dream depends upon a "far deeper doubleness, her wish and her fear that doubleness won't work, that she will have to settle for just one thing: one intrusive, penetrating, possessive lover" (9). In a psychoanalytic context, the adolescent Hermia is working out with Lysander a much earlier, more formative relationship with someone not seen or even mentioned in the play: her mother.

So much for the first phase of psychoanalytical criticism which, according to Holland, was practiced in that mode for two main reasons: either to use the insight of the dramatist to confirm the views of the scientist, or to use the ideas of the scientist to understand what the dramatist was doing. The problem there is that both approaches regard Hermia's dream as if it were a real dream, rather than as an artifact. In the 1960s and 1970s, psychoanalytical critics shifted their stance. No longer did they treat Hermia like a literary adolescent, a real person; instead, they fit her and her dream into the fabric of the total play. Holland cites two Shakespeareans who have taken that approach: Marjorie Garber, who argues that Hermia should not be afraid of ambiguity or double meanings, since that is what the play is all about; and Melvin D. Faber, who regards the dream as fulfilling Hermia's wish for sex with Lysander and thus part of "Shakespeare's effort to establish masculine control over unruly impulses associated with the lack of proper boundaries between male and female" (Faber 1972, 11).[13] Holland believes that the questions of separation and fusion in Hermia's dream permeate the entire play. All of the couples, including Theseus and Hippolyta and Oberon and Titania, endure separations of various durations and cruelty, but all are reconciled and brought together by the play's end.

More recently, psychoanalytically oriented critics have become interested in extending the foregoing kinds of analyses to establish a self-structuring relation with the text, one that would include personal feelings of the reader and the quality of his or her own interpretation of the play. Instead of searching for a definitive reading, these critics now accept ways of talking about the personal quality of response. In short, they have developed an identity theory that they call "transactive criticism." These critics actively create, or transact, the material with which they are dealing.

By engaging in transactive criticism, Holland brings his own associations to Hermia's dream and its context, which involves "a rather uncomfortable hovering between different views of love" (15). One view sees love as a total, consuming desire; another is less demanding, admitting of a change of heart, or appetite. Holland then explores related views of love that Hermia's dream and *A Midsummer Night's Dream* as a whole have aroused in his consciousness. Since his analysis is highly personal, or subjective, he naturally uses the first-person singular when speaking about what he thinks and feels. Despite his own feelings about love, he asserts that the play rejects possessiveness, but he notes the paradox that the unions of the lovers—their becoming "eternally" knit—follow a series of separations and infidelities. He is uncomfortable, he admits, because he fails to see how infidelity leads to fidelity. He confesses that the play's open-endedness—its silence on how trust is finally created among the young couples—relates to something in himself: his need to *know* things, to feel certain, especially about human relations (17–18). This—a willingness to assert something about oneself, making explicit what was only implicit in earlier psychoanalytic criticism—demonstrates the new direction taken by this kind of criticism.

GENDER CRITICISM

Gender criticism, or what used to be called feminist criticism, arose in the United States partly as a result of the civil rights movement of the 1950s and 1960s. Insofar as it tries to understand the nature of woman and the relationships between the sexes, it also derives directly or indirectly from some aspects of psychoanalytical criticism, with which it is closely associated.[14] The practitioners of gender criticism are not usually psychoanalysts themselves, but many are well informed about various modes of psychoanalysis, whether or not they take a specifically designated psychoanalytical approach to their subject. Freud and his perceived bias against women is of course the bête noire of these critics, who have attempted to found a more evenhanded critique of sexuality and of gender relations.

Patriarchy is the other and older nemesis. Much of gender criticism is directed against patriarchal structures in literature as in life—against, that is, male domination of the female. Recent scholarship has shown, however, that in the early modern period—the period when Shakespeare wrote *A Midsummer Night's Dream*—the situation was more complicated than a simple, reductionist view of patriarchy makes it appear. Women had their own way of challenging male authority, then as now.[15] Although Titania's challenge to Oberon's authority ends in failure, the fact that she could oppose it so directly and openly, and then lose only through his stealthy magic, indicates Shakespeare's high regard for female strength of character.[16]

In the introduction to *The Woman's Part* (1980), one of the first anthologies of feminist criticism (as it was then called), the editors begin by defining their subject. Feminist criticism "pays acute attention to the woman's part in literature. But it is not only and not always feminocentric, for it examines both men and women and the social structures that shape them."[17] More than two decades later, much of this agenda has been accomplished, but gender studies—with or without a particular point of view—remain important. They have opened new avenues of research and understanding in Shakespearean studies that can be and frequently are fruitful and rewarding.

In "*A Midsummer Night's Dream*: 'Jack Shall Have Jill; / Naught Shall Go Ill,' " Shirley Nelson Garner maintains that the movement of the play toward ordering the fairy, human, and natural worlds also moves toward satisfying the men's psychological needs, but at a cost of disrupting women's bonds with each other.[18] She considers the conflict between Oberon and Titania regarding possession of the Indian boy, which has caused chaos in the natural world. She claims that Titania's attachment to the boy is "clearly erotic" and ultimately is her link to the mortal woman she loved (129). Oberon's desire for the boy shows that he, too, is attracted to him as well as jealous of him; he demands Titania's exclusive love. Noting that Oberon's wish to have the boy is consistent with the Renaissance practice of removing a male child from the care of women to prepare him for manhood, Garner argues that, notwithstanding, the text gives no evidence that Oberon really wants to groom the child for adulthood as a man. Besides, he has no intention of returning the changeling child to his father, where he might more properly be reared for that purpose. If winning the boy from Titania lies at the center of the play, Oberon succeeds by humiliating and cruelly treating Titania. He gains both the boy and the exclusive love and obedience of his queen, but at her considerable cost.

Like Oberon, Theseus and Egeus want the exclusive love of a woman and her obedience, but, Garner claims, they want this to accommodate their homoerotic desires. These she defines as "unconsummated homosexual feelings, which may or may not be recognized" (141, n. 8). Here Garner probably overstates the case, at least in regard to Theseus, although she cites some good evidence to show Egeus's feelings for Demetrius, both at the beginning and later on, even after the young couples have been rightly sorted out. As for Theseus, the best argument Garner makes is that in Hippolyta he has found a woman who, as an Amazonian warrior, is not traditionally feminine. "Her androgynous character appears to resolve for Theseus the apparent dissociation of his romantic life, the sign of which is his continual desertion of women who love him" (133). In addition, since on Shakespeare's stage the actors playing

Theseus and Hippolyta were both male, they must have looked more like homosexual rather than heterosexual lovers.

From there Garner goes on to state that whereas the separation of Hippolyta and Titania from other women is implied, "the breaking of women's bonds is central in the plot involving the four young lovers" (136). The quarrel between Hermia and Helena is more demeaning than that between the men. Moreover, once Demetrius and Lysander no longer compete for the same woman, their enmity apparently vanishes. However, after the women are given over to the men whom they will marry, they are permanently separated. "Once their friendship is undermined and their power diminished, they are presumably 'ready' for marriage" (136). While the text does not show them either reconciled to each other or still hostile, they have nothing to say to each other after they are awakened in 4.1, and say nothing at all in act 5. For Garner, this amounts to a "portentous silence." In their new roles as wives, their silence suggests that they will be obedient and allow their husbands to dominate. Although the ending of the play may appear fully joyous, and "the prospect of love, peace, safety, and prosperity . . . as promising as it will ever be," at least in any Shakespearean comedy, the cost of this harmony is the restoration of patriarchal hierarchy. For Garner, the return to the old order—that is, the order as it was at the outset of the play—depends upon the end of the women's solidarity and their utter submission to men.

In her chapter on "The Play in Its Time: Female Power," Helen Hackett combines a feminist analysis of *A Midsummer Night's Dream* with a New Historical approach.[19] Here, I shall discuss only the former. Like other critics, she recognizes how the *Dream* shows that subjugation to male rulers and spouses is "a more natural state of affairs than unbridled female autonymy" (25). She notes that, although mothers are mostly absent from the play, two are mentioned, if only to be marginalized and excluded. One is Thisbe's mother, who at first has a part in the play-within-the-play but never appears. (The role is originally assigned to Starveling in 1.2, but he comes on instead as Moonshine in act 5.) The other is the Indian boy's mother, whom Titania describes in her pregnancy (2.1.125–34). Hackett contrasts that description with Theseus's lecture to Hermia on filial disobedience (1.1.47–51), where conception is figured "as the quasi-divine act of a male progenitor alone, justifying absolute paternal authority" (28). According to Hackett, Titania's speech, one of the richest passages in the text, calls attention to the significance of gender: "Titania and the votaress are emphatically female, and the merchant ships [in her description] are the vehicles of men's exploits and adventures" (29). The ships are made to seem "inconsequential," their sails hollow and filled with wind, as compared with the image of female fertility on the shore, heavy with the burden of life. This is the most serious challenge to male authority in the play, "the only truly equivalent force" (29).

Hackett further contrasts this image of Titania's "voluptuosly and magnificently pregnant" votaress with the portrait of the imperial vota-ress described by Oberon later (2.1.155–64). The latter is "chaste, watery, ethereal," however much revered for her chastity. But that very chastity is at odds with the main theme of *A Midsummer Night's Dream*, which is to celebrate married love and the progeny that such unions may pro-duce. Identified with the moon, the imperial votaress is a mysterious and nearly divine figure, but also "chilly, insipid and dampening," as com-pared with the "generous materiality," "fullness," and "merriment" of Titania's votaress (29–30). If self-willed female desire threatens the pa-triarchal order represented in the play, becoming a serious source of conflict, as in Hermia's defiance of her father and Titania's of Oberon, the resolution of the struggle is "the realignment of female sexuality with patriarchy, not its denial" (30).

Christy Desmet takes a different view of the significance of Theseus's speech. His elaboration on the horrors of becoming a nun inadvertently raises questions about the joys of marriage.[20] Although Theseus empha-sizes the convent's constraints, where nuns are forced to live in cloisters and are sexually deprived, their "maiden pilgrimage" nonetheless affords them with a metaphorical freedom to wander. They do not have to fit their fancies to a father's will. If they chant their hymns to a cold and fruitless moon, they do so in the out-of-doors. Married life looks less perfect by comparison.

Furthermore,

> By involving Hermia in the humanist rhetoric of friendship, advising her to marry rather than subjecting her directly to the harsh law of the father, Theseus not only grants Hermia the status of a speaking subject, which the law itself would deny her, but he implicitly li-censes her to revise the masculine tropes that configure the discourse of romantic love and marriage. (Desmet 1998, 310)

This she does immediately afterward in her dialogue with Lysander when the others depart. Later, in the forest and lost, Hermia is able to counter

Lysander's advances, using a wider range of rhetorical styles than he can muster. As regards Helena and Demetrius, also lost in the forest, the struggle for rhetorical supremacy is more pronounced and results in their language becoming polarized. "Helena's speech is rich with ornament, Demetrius's the unmediated voice of physical menace" (312). For reasons that Desmet explains, Helena's rhetoric has an emasculating effect on Demetrius.

While a good measure of "disfiguring" women, or the attempt to disfigure, occurs in the *Dream*, women also do some disfiguring "by usurping the public rhetoric that humanist educators fashioned to strengthen the community of men" (Desmet 1998, 314). They exploit rhetoric's ability to fuse voice and vision. They also fashion an alternative ethics, producing and controlling the poetic "music" of *A Midsummer Night's Dream*. By "stepping out of their texts and speaking up," they "offer a feminist poetics that transforms their political usurpation of humanist rhetoric into an ethical act" (315).

According to Desmet, Titania functions as the voice of ethical commitment. While the first two acts of the play contrast the relative rights of fathers and mothers, the two plots "merge to offer a unified defense of female sexual sovereignty, the woman's rights over her own body and soul" (317). Like Hermia, Titania defends her retention of the Indian boy to Oberon "as if in a public forum." Her speech locates the boy "within an ethically and poetically superior matriarchy that reinforces her regal and maternal rights to him." She claims that only death, and not sexual infidelity or all she owns, can disrupt the company of women (318). Furthermore, she balances her feelings for female solidarity with criticism of her own marriage. She takes her stand, Desmet concludes, "by renouncing the comfort of rhetorical figures," and by engaging in rhetorical disfigurement, she becomes the most ethical speaker in the play (319–20).

In "The (In)significance of 'Lesbian' Desire in Early Modern England," Valerie Traub takes the discussion of female friendship discussed in the preceding chapter a giant step further. She also compares the relationsip between Hermia and Helena with that of Rosalind and Celia in *As You Like It* and notes that, for these two pairs of female characters, "the initial erotic investment is in one another."[21] Their dialogues with each other, she claims, are "as erotically compelling as anything spoken in the heterosexual moments in these comedies." She calls attention, for instance, to Celia's speech at 1.3.71–74 which describes how she and Rosalind have slept together and, like Juno's swans, were inseparable, and to Le Beau's comment about their love "as dearer than the natural bond of sisters" (1.2.265). In *A Midsummer Night's Dream*, Lysander's "seductive come-on" at 2.2.42 is "qualitatively, emotionally, physically" no different from Helena's speech later on recalling the closeness she and Hermia shared as friends (157–58).

Like Garner, Traub focuses on the divorce of female unity, but she contends that "the relative power of each woman is aligned according to her *denial* of homoerotic bonds" (158). The breakup of the union between women is something regrettably betrayed and lost. "It is the female, rather than the male characters of these plays, who, by their silent denial of the other woman's emotional claims, position homoerotic desire in the past" (158). The eradication of homoerotic desire, as between Hermia and Helena, is replicated in the Titania-Oberon plot. The little Indian boy is representative not only of Titania's female order, but also of female-oriented erotic bonds. He is "the manifest link between of a prior, homoerotic affection between women that doesn't so much exclude Oberon as render him temporarily superfluous" (159). Thus affronted, Oberon moves to humiliate Titania erotically by making her fall in love with a monster and then surrender the child to him, making the boy henceforward secure for purely masculine purposes.

Traub's summing up of the situation is worth quoting at length, since it relates, on the one hand, to psychoanalytical interpretations and, on the other hand, to an ultra-feminist viewpoint.

> The gendered and erotic scenarios enacted in these plays do not exemplify psychosexual *necessity*—that is, a developmental movement through progressive erotic stages—but an economic, political imperative: as each woman is resecured in the patriarchal, reproductive order, her desires are made to conform to her "place." Significantly, the homoerotic desires of these female characters existed comfortably within the patriarchal order until the onset of marriage; it is only with the cementing of male bonds through the exchange of women, or, in Titania's case, the usurpation of the right to formalize bonds through the bodies of others, that the independent desires of female bodies become a focus of male anxiety and heterosexual retribution. (159)

NEW HISTORICISM AND CULTURAL MATERIALISM

Since New Historicism and Cultural Materialism share similar critical approaches to literature, it is appropriate to consider them together in this section. Terence Hawkes discusses these similarities and contrasts both to the old historical approach, which tends to use history primarily as the background for works of literature. In so doing, the older historicism privileged literature. The New Historicism has attempted to forge a new relationship between history and literature, radically readjusting the balance so that literature does not enjoy its hitherto privileged position.

> On the one hand, it [the New Historicism] represents a reaction against an a-historical or "idealist" view of the world in which an apparently free-floating and autonomous body of writing called "literature" serves as the repository of the universal values of a supposedly "human nature." On the other, it constitutes a rejection of the presuppositions of a "history of ideas" which tends to regard literature as a static mirror of its time. Its "newness" lies precisely in its determination to reposition "literature" altogether, to perceive literary texts as active constituent *elements* and *aspects* of their time, participants in, not mirrors, of it; respondent to and involved with numerous other enterprises, such as law, marriage, religion, and government, all engaged in the productions of "texts" and, as a result, of the cultural meanings that finally constitute a way of life.[22]

Louis Adrian Montrose's chapter "*A Midsummer Night's Dream* and the Shaping Fantasies of Elizabeth Culture: Gender, Power, Form,"[23] is a good exemplar of the New Historicism, which often begins with an anecdote or similar narrative that places the work of literature in its cultural matrix. Montrose's chapter begins with Simon Forman's erotic dream in 1597 of walking with a queen, "a little elderly woman in a coarse white petticoat all unready" (65). In Montrose's interpretation, the figure of the queen represents Forman's mother, who was still alive at the time. It also can represent the aged Queen Elizabeth, and Montrose links that aspect of the dream both to the cult of Elizabeth that had grown up during her reign and to the images of the queen as recorded in various descriptions during the last decade of the century.

Montrose's aim was not to psychoanalyze Forman but to emphasize "the historical specificity of the psychological process" (66). He considers the connection of Queen Elizabeth with the play's first performances, not to accept or reject them, but to suggest that the queen's "pervasive *cultural presence* was a condition of the play's imaginative possibility" (69). *A Midsummer Night's Dream* was "a new *production* of Elizabethan culture, enlarging the dimensions of the cultural field and altering the lines of force within it" (69). Montrose proceeds to demonstrate this thesis in the ensuing pages, invoking Elizabethan interest in Amazons as well as various attitudes toward Elizabeth herself and especially her status as a virgin queen.

Space here does not permit an extended analysis of Montrose's argument, but suffice it to say that he amply shows how the structure of the *Dream* "eventually restores the inverted Amazonian system of gender and nurture to a patriarchal norm" (72). Montrose considers carefully and in detail the opposing notions of the father as *genitor* and *pater* (biological and social father) and the mother as *genetrix* and *mater* in the contrasting speeches of Theseus (1.1.47–51) and Titania (2.1.123–37). Even in Titania's speech, Shakespeare's "embryological notions" remain "distinctly Aristotelian," or phallocentric: the mother is represented as "a *vessel*, as a container for her son; she is not his *maker*" (75). The two speeches formulate a proposition about the genesis of gender and power: "men make women, and they make themselves through the medium of women" (75–76).

Montrose also explores the interplay between sexual politics in the Elizabethan family and sexual politics in the Elizabethan monarchy. Here the Amazonian metaphor becomes significant, although it was never popular among Elizabethan encomiasts, particularly since the queen herself did not like the comparisons of herself to an Amazonian ruler. Poets Sir Walter Raleigh and Edmund Spenser had to tread carefully when employing the metaphor (78–79). Montrose gives as an example Spenser's conjoining "the amazons huge river" and "fruitfullest Virginia" (*The Faerie Queene*, II, Proem 2) to invoke not only two regions of the New World, but "two archetypes of Elizabeth culture: the engulfing Amazon and the nurturing Virgin" (79). Later in the same book, Spenser conjoins them again in Belphoebe, the virgin huntress. "The female body—and, in particular, the symbolic body of the queen—provides a cognitive map for Elizabethan culture," according to Montrose, "a matrix for the Elizabethan power are played out" (79). *A Midsummer Night's Dream*, accordingly, is permeated by images and devices that reflect Elizabethan court culture, as in Oberon's speech at 2.1.156–68, where "the public and domestic domains of Elizabethan culture intersect in the figure of the imperial votaress" (83).

Like Spenser and other courtly writers, Montrose contends, Shakespeare

splits the triune Elizabethan cult image between the fair vestal, an
unattainable *virgin*; and the fairy queen, an intractable *wife* and a
dominating *mother*. Oberon uses one against the other in order to
reassert male prerogatives. Thus in the logic of its structure, Shakespeare's comedy symbolically neutralizes the royal power to which
it ostensibly pays homage. (84)

For this reason and others, Montrose argues that the *absence* of Elizabeth, not her actual presence at performances of the *Dream*, was as important as her *"cultural presence."*

Another New Historicist treatment of the *Dream* is found in Theodore
B. Leinwand's essay " 'I Believe We Must Leave the Killing Out': Deference and Accommodation in *A Midsummer Night's Dream*."[24] Part of
Leinwand's purpose is to show not only the mechanicals' concern with
strategies of accommodation as regards performing before the nobility,
but also the playwright's, William Shakespeare's, similar concern. "The
power of spectators like Theseus and Elizabeth to give meaning to command performances," he asserts, "weighed heavily on playwrights and
actors" (145). It certainly weighs heavily on Bottom and his fellow thespians, as shown in the dialogue in 1.2 and especially 3.1. And with good
cause, although, as Leinwand reveals, accommodation and negotiation
could replace severe punishment for perceived offenses in Elizabethan
England. Nevertheless, the 1590s were a period of both social and economic disorder, due to a failing harvest, high food prices, low wages,
war with Spain, and the queen's aging rule; and the burden of these
disorders fell most heavily upon the lower classes, including artisans and
tradesmen (147–53).

At all levels, below as well as above, the desire was to prevent disorder
as much as possible. Deference and accommodation could accomplish a
good deal and "slow down traffic at the gallows" (Leinwand 1998, 152).
Parliament and other government bodies joined with the local poor and
artisans to deal with dearth, adopting a paternalistic attitude. According
to Leinwand, this paternalism was inherent in Elizabethan social policy
and "is writ large across the relationships in *A Midsummer Night's
Dream*" along with deference and accommodation (153). When Theseus
rejects the other pretenders to entertainment, which involve battle, riot,
and rage, preferring instead Quince's play, he reflects Elizabethan opposition to violent threats. His willingness to compensate for the artisans'
shortcomings in performance (5.1.89–105, 210–15) likewise reflects

Elizabeth's rule, which usually tried to go part way to meet the artisans' demands in times of need.

Like any good other New Historicist, Leinwand brings a quantity of historical detail to establish these points in relation to Shakespeare's play. He then moves to determine the extent to which Shakespeare accommodated himself, and was accommodated, to those in power during the period of composition and performance of *A Midsummer Night's Dream*. Adopting Walter Cohen's view that Shakespeare's theater took "a fundamentally artisanal historical form,"[25] Leinwand proposes an admittedly oversimplified analogy: the mechanicals' play in *Dream* is to the dominant Athenian culture, as represented by Theseus and his court, as the London artisans' play is to Elizabeth and her court. For example, the four lovers' marriage plans and the attention they receive in Theseus's court glance at marriage brokering in Elizabeth's court and her readiness to intervene whenever it suited her to do so. For another example, Shakespeare's company and others like it were compelled to accommodate themselves to numerous restrictions on playing, such as the prohibitions against personal satire, representation of religious controversy, and criticism of court policies. Many plays, however, managed to evade such restrictions. "Playwrights deferred and yet criticized, and both City and Court responded with tolerance at one moment [like Theseus's tolerance of Quince's prologue], imprisonment at another" (160).[26]

Like the New Historicism, Cultural Materialism declines to privilege literature, but its approach takes a somewhat different path. While both concern themselves with social and political issues and the role of drama in the public theaters, New Historicists tend to see Shakespeare's plays as reinforcing the dominant order, whereas Cultural Materialists tend to interrogate them "to the point of subversion."[27] In "Or," his chapter on *A Midsummer Night's Dream*,[28] Hawkes begins by examining the name "Nedar," which appears twice in the dialogue with reference to Helena's parentage (1.1.107 and 4.1.129). Although most critics assume that "Nedar" must be her father,[29] Hawkes makes the point that no evidence appears, either in the play or in the antecedents of the name in history and myth, to determine whether in fact Nedar is Helena's mother or father. It could as well be her mother, and if so, she is yet another of the elderly ladies, like Lysander's dowager aunt, to name just one of many, who people the play if only as shadowy figures (225–26). Hawkes links these references to "the pervasive cultural presence" of Queen Elizabeth referred to by Montrose in his essay. Hawkes notes that "Nedar" is an anagram of "Arden," which was Shakespeare's mother's family name (227).

Although the definition of motherhood was a crucial concern in Elizabethan culture as in all cultures, *A Midsummer Night's Dream* curiously marginalizes "the nurturing, vessel-like relationship of mother to child, which traditionally tempers the inseminating, constitutive and 'imprinting' role of the father" (227). The Amazonian matriarchy, which made the mother-daughter relationship fundamental in its society, is presumably vanquished along with Hippolyta, its queen, by Theseus. This appears implicit in the duke's support of Egeus's claim regarding his daughter Hermia. "Whatever else the plays has on offer, it is certainly not the delights or consolations of motherhood" (228).

Hawkes continues by examining the text of *Dream* in considerable detail, exploring many of its indeterminacies and relating them to the cultural, social, and political situations of the late sixteenth century. He notes how an Ovidean principle seems to lie at the play's heart and comments on how change springs from

> the very stratagems designed to maintain sameness, to the dismay of those caught up in the process. The very idea of filial generation, for example, whereby a father "imprints" a "form in wax," deals in an evident sense of repetition through the metaphor of "reproduction," and its striking links with "printing" and "reprinting." (235)

But Egeus discovers that parents cannot depend upon repeating themselves in their children when they decide to make liaisons "in the world beyond the family" (235). Hawkes thus describes the paradox "whereby the process of filiation, committed to an 'imprinting' repetition of the same, inevitably leads on to a social process of affiliation, through marriage in this case, which must, willy-nilly, be committed to difference" (235).

In a section of his essay titled "Wall," Hawkes treats the subject of transgression as it emerges in *A Midsummer Night's Dream* and notes a further paradox: "a wall intended for breaching must generate a fundamental contradiction" (241). Contradictions linking violence and affection abound in the play, from Theseus's wooing with his sword and winning love through injuries to Egeus's treatment of Hermia and Oberon's of Titania. Hawkes cites Steven Mullaney's work on Elizabethan theaters and their location beyond the city's walls. "By 1599, the city was ringed with playhouses, but the flight of the theaters from the city centre to its margins demanded to be seen metaphorically as a flight to liberty, not banishment" (242–43). Indeed, those locations were referred to as the "liberties." What the city fathers feared was the political dimension of audience participation, or the impulse to it, that theatrical representation induces, as may be seen in the enactment of the play-within-the-play in *Dream*.

Marxist criticism is closely allied to Cultural Materialism; in fact, in many respects it is its progenitor. In "Bottom's Dream, the Lion's Roar, and Hostility of Class Difference in *A Midsummer Night's Dream*," Michael Schneider gives a classical Marxist interpretation of class conflict in Shakespeare's play.[30] He argues that the text offers "concrete support for reading class struggle as a present absence" (193) and adduces a number of examples to support this reading. All the while he admits that Shakespeare was no "proto-Marxist" (205); rather, a class-conscious rendering of the text reveals that it is only beneath the "polite surface" of the play that one may find many aggressive gestures to validate his interpretation.

Schneider's many examples come from the language of the rude mechanicals, which he characterizes as containing indications of submerged aggression typical of class resentment. "It is as if the text itself enacts an effort at repression or self-control that nevertheless, perversely and subversely, reveals itself in spite of itself" (200). His analysis of the first part of Quince's prologue to "Pyramus and Thisbe" in act 5 is his main illustration of this point, although he offers a number of other examples as well. Schneider maintains that "[a]t each turn of phrase class resentment and aggression undercut what appears on the surface as an obsequious desire to please" (200). Of course Quince gets his punctuation wrong, as Theseus recognizes, but Schneider's point is nonetheless clear:

> If we offend, it is with our good will
> > That you should think we come not to offend,
> But with good will. (5.1.108–10)

Schneider goes on to argue that the text also reveals an ideological threat in the form of sexual aggression. He cites the lion's roar itself as suggesting sexual threat—a threat to the ladies that Bottom and the others recognize well enough, if not its sexual implications (3.1.21–26). Similarly, Bottom is concerned about the effect of his sword, which as Pyramus he must use to kill himself. Schneider claims that this concern echoes the "patriarchal phallicness" of Theseus's wooing Hippolyta (201). Moreover, Bottom's transformation into an ass, or an ass's head, provides "a powerful symbolic image of working class ethos" as well as a ludicrous visual effect (201). The ass, after all, as a beast of burden, suggests subjugation to a master as well as strength and endurance, which contrast strikingly with "the leisure and self-indulgence of the aristocrats in the play" (201).

In his discussion of Bottom as the ass, Schneider brings in pertinent references to Shakespeare's likely source in Apuleius's *The Golden Ass* and develops the submerged implications of Bottom's cuckolding of Oberon in his night with Titania (202). Finally, Bottom's bergomask is "a rustic dance arising from folk tradition that expresses the working-class spirit of festival" (205). While it concludes the play-within-the-play, it does not end the play proper. That is left for Puck and the other fairies. But significantly, Puck introduces that final part of the last scene with a reference once more to a hungry lion roaring (5.1.349).

Postcolonial literary criticism may be considered a subset of the New Historicism insofar as it concerns itself with the analysis of texts written about colonized countries by writers from the colonizing culture using a historical perspective. Typically, postcolonial criticism is about texts that deal with Third World countries previously colonized by Western powers. A more generalized view of this critical approach, however, accepts any criticism that focuses on colonizing tendencies by any powers anywhere. Margo Hendricks's " 'Obscured by Dreams': Race, Empire, and Shakespeare's *A Midsummer Night's Dream*"[31] thus fits into this category nicely.

Hendricks asks why the changeling boy is an Indian; why, from a cultural standpoint, do the fairies fight for possession of him; and what implications about race and Tudor England's "mercantile or colonialist/ imperialist ideology" (41) may be inferred from Shakespeare's use of India. The basis of her argument is "that the figurative evocation of India localizes Shakespeare's characterization of the fairies in *A Midsummer Night's Dream* and marks the play's complicity in the racialist ideologies being created by early modern England's participation in imperialism" (43). She contends that this racialist ideology is not unique to Shakespeare's play but commonplace among many other representations of India during the period.

Hendricks surveys at length the travel literature of the time and shows how Shakespeare's dramatic invention "intersects with lexical formulation in the reconceptualization of race" (43). For example, she analyzes

Lewes Vertomannus's account of his travels in India, as translated by Richard Eden in his *History of Travayle in the West and East Indies* (1577). In particular, she notes the extraordinary sexual mores of India as well as its reported wealth and fruitfulness (49–50). India is "a world where an Amazon and a fairy king can be lovers; a site where exoticism and difference are as conventional as trade and commodities" (51). India, morever, can become "the center of linguistic and ideological exchanges between Athens and fairyland" (52). Titania's speech describing the Indian boy's mother (2.1.123–37) reflects the idealized imagery of travel literature; her speech, rich with the language of English mercantilism, evokes the power of traders to exploit India (53). In the *Dream*, Shakespeare's poetic geography becomes "the commodified space of a racialized feminine eroticism that . . . paradoxically excited and threatened the masculinity of European traders" (53).

Despite what other critics have argued, Hendricks disagrees that Oberon's interest in the Indian boy is paternal. It is, rather, "a perceived prerogative to claim possession—to have 'all . . . tied to' him" (53). Oberon desires the boy, in other words, as "an exotic emblem of [his] worldly authority" (54). This does not, however, fully answer the question of the boy's Indian ethnicity, which Hendricks finds in the larger issue of gender relations in the play. Maintaining that change, or transformation, is central to the dramatic plot and to the resolution of the quarrel between between Oberon and Titania, Hendricks notes the transformation of Bottom as a substitute for the Indian boy in Titania's affections. Oberon thus supplies a changeling for a changeling. Bottom also becomes a substitute for Oberon in Titania's affections. These changes, Hendricks contends, "literally and symbolically" register "an ethnic (or racial) change that involves the forcible removal of a person from one culture to another" (55). At the center of what Hendricks calls "this trope of change" is a concept that is linked to the Spanish concept of *mestizaje*, or mixedness (55). Both Bottom and the changeling boy represent a hybrid, or mixed, state.[32]

Titania's refusal to surrender the Indian boy to Oberon, according to Hendricks, may echo an Indian woman's challenge (in one of Vertomannus's tales) to "Eurocentric, patriarchal assumptions about control of the female body and about that body's ability to destabilize the idea of marking race solely through paternity" (58). Hendricks further suggests that Oberon's uneasiness about Bottom in Titania's bower coupled with her fondness for the changeling boy "resonates with the European's growing anxiety about the definition of race in the borderlands. . . . What we witness in India and fairyland is the fragmentation of patriarchal ideologies denoting race because women's erotic desires can displace and dispel the sexual continuum upon which race is constituted" (58).

All this leads Hendricks to conclude that the concept of race, at least as it emerges from *A Midsummer Night's Dream*, must be rewritten to include "an ideology capable of handling the superficial differences between Indians and Europeans" (58). Bottom's removal from fairyland, as well as the Indian boy's removal from Titania's bower, may alleviate Oberon's vexation, but it does not dispel the racial problems caused by their existence. Bottom's return to his human form and to Athens restores a class and gender hierarchy, but it leaves behind

> a new vision of a racial landscape, a "new world" where the image of humanity is not the European but a changeling. . . . More important, Shakespeare's two changelings in *A Midsummer Night's Dream* are haunted by the ghostly presence of the historical condition of *mestizaje* which occasions both Shakespeare's dramatic representation of India and the modern Western notion of race. (59)

MYTH AND ARCHETYPAL CRITICISM

One of the earliest advocates and practitioners of myth and archetypal criticism was Maud Bodkin, whose *Archetypal Patterns in Poetry: Psychological Studies of the Imagination* (1934) drew upon the theories of Carl Jung and Gilbert Murray. She studied the way in which certain themes, especially in tragedy, show a persistence with the life of a community or race and compared the different forms they assumed. More recently, Northrop Frye developed the approach in "Archetypal Criticism: Theory of Myths," the third chapter of his monumental work, *Anatomy of Criticism* (1957). He begins his study of archetypes with the world of myth, which he defines as "an abstract or purely literary world of fictional and thematic design, unaffected by canons of plausible adaptation to familiar experience." The meaning or pattern of poetry is "a structure of imagery with conceptual implications."[33] This type of criticism has clear links to the analysis of image patterns that once was a favorite approach of critics but has since been surpassed by other approaches. Frye's approach, however, extends well beyond the analysis of patterns of imagery to larger and more significant patterns.

Frye distinguishes four basic patterns of myth in literature and relates them to the four seasons: spring (comedy), summer (romance), autumn (tragedy), and winter (irony and satire). Here, we are concerned only with comedy, or the mythos of comedy, whose tendency is, according to Frye, to incorporate the hero and heroine into society, the basis of most comedy from ancient classical times to the present.[34] "At the beginning of the play the obstructing characters are in charge of the play's society. . . . At the end of the play the device in the plot that brings hero and heroine together causes a new society to crystallize around the hero."[35] Frye, however, recognizes other possibilities in comedy: society may not change sufficiently to embrace the hero but remain demonic; it may begin to change but continue to remain repressed by the older society; or the older society may be restored, renewed, idealized, or reborn.[36] In *A Midsummer Night's Dream*, the society over which Theseus rules changes at least sufficiently to allow the young couples under his charge to join with him in wedding festivities, and in fairyland the old order over which Oberon rules is renewed. Or, as Frye puts in in *A Natural Perspective*, in *Dream* "the action moves from a world of parental tyranny and irrational law into a forest. There the comic resolution is attained, and the cast returns with it into their former world."[37]

In addition, the comic drive is "a drive toward identity."[38] It manifests itself in three ways:

> There is a plural or social identity, when a new social group crystallizes around the marriage of the hero and heroine in the final moments of the comedy. There is dual or erotic identity, when the hero and heroine get married. And there is individual identity, when a character comes to know himself in a way that he did not before. (118)

In *A Midsummer Night's Dream*, the social group is not new so much as revitalized by the marriages at the end of the play; and although Shakespeare does not dive deeply into the characters of the several couples, they seem to know themselves better after their experience in the forest. If the phases of comedy are charted as stages "in an ascent from the demonic towards the apocoplyptic," they may be seen as moving "from things as they are to things as they should be, from bondage to freedom, unhappiness to festivity, alienation to a growing awareness of a regained identity."[39]

Frye's most famous formulation of the mythos of comedy is his concept, using a phrase borrowed from John Keats's *Endymion*, of "the drama of the green world." "The action of the comedy begins in a world represented as a normal world, moves into the green world, goes into a metamorphosis there in which the comic resolution is achieved, and returns to the normal world."[40] The "normal world," which frustrates desire, is demonic; the "green world," which permits satisfaction of desire, becomes apocolyptic. This polarizing action of the two worlds relates comedy to myth, ritual, and dream, insofar as the "green world charges the comedies with the symbolism of the victory of summer over winter" and has analogies "to the dream world that we create out of our own desires."[41] This, clearly, is the action of *A Midsummer Night's Dream*.

In *Shakespeare's Festive Comedy*, C. L. Barber approaches the archetypal stucture of comedy from a different standpoint, that of what he calls "saturnalian comedy." The saturnalian pattern "appears in many variations, all of which involve inversion, statement and counterstatement, and a basic movement which can be summarized in the formula, through release to clarification."[42] In regard to *A Midsummer Night's Dream*, Barber suggests,

> The whole night's action is presented as a release of shaping fantasy which brings clarification about the tricks of strong imagination. We watch a dream; but we are awake, thanks to a pervasive humor about the tendency to take fantasy literally, whether in love, in superstition, or in Bottom's mechanical dramatics. . . . [T]he folly of fantasy becomes a general subject, echoes back and forth between the strains of the play's imitative counterpoint. (124)

Barber considers first the young lovers, then the fairies, and finally the broad comedy of the clowns, or rude mechanicals. He notes correctly that Theseus and Hippolyta are "principals without being protagonists; the play happens for them rather than to them" (125). Theseus's direction for festivities to Philostrate in 1.1 is abruptly interrupted by Egeus's complaint: "After the initial invocation of nuptial festivity, we are confronted by the sort of tension from which merriment is a release" (125). The woods provide an escape from parental inhibitions and the organized community. This sense of release is prepared for by the dialogue between Lysander and Hermia who, left alone, mention the tragic possibilities of passion (1.1.135–49). They shake free of these thoughts by planning their escape.

Unlike some of Shakespeare's later comic characters, such as Perdita and Florizel in *The Winter's Tale*, the young lovers in *Dream* lack the awareness or consciousness of their situation as evidenced by their lack of qualifying irony. The result is that they are "rather dull and undignified," according to Barber (128). "The life in the lovers' parts is not to be caught in individual speeches, but by regarding the whole movement of the farce, which swings and spins each in turn through a common pattern, an evolution that seems to have an impersonal power of its own" (128). This farce not only puts them beside themselves but takes them beyond themselves, with little suggestion, however, that involves a growth in insight, except in one instance. When Hermia and Helena begin their fierce quarrel, breaking the "double-cherry" bond that once united them, they "move from the loyalties of one stage of life to those of another" (130). The pageant that Puck comments upon (3.2.114–15) is "fond," that is, foolish, because "the mortals do not realize that they are in it, nor that it is sure to come out right, since nature will have its way" (131).

Barber is very perceptive with respect to nature and to the ritual of May games as suggested by the action of *A Midsummer Night's Dream.*

> Shakespeare, in developing a May-game action at length to express the will in nature that is consummated in marriage, brings out underlying magical meanings of the ritual while keeping always a sense of what it is humanly, as an experience. . . . Poetry conveys the experience of amorous tendency diffused in nature; and poetry, dance, gesture, dramatic fiction, combine to create, in the fairies, creatures who embody the passionate mind's elated sense of its own omnipotence. The woods are established as a region of metamorphosis, where in liquid moonlight or glimmering starlight, things can change, merge and melt into each other. Metamorphosis expresses both what love sees and what it seeks to do. (132)

This aptly summarizes the action of Shakespeare's play and its significance. In analyzing what happens to Titania, for instance, Barber asserts that when she finds a new object to exchange for the child, she experiences a change of heart "that contributes to what is consummated in marriage, this one a part of the rhythm of adult life, as opposed to the change in the young lovers that goes with growing up. Once Titania has made this transition, their ritual marriage is renewed" (137).

As for the mechanicals, in their preparation for and presentation of "Pyramus and Thisbe," "Shakespeare captures the naiveté of folk dramatics and makes it serve his controlling purpose as a final variant of imaginative aberration" (151). The comedy lies not in what is acted so much as in the performers' failure to translate actor into character. Bottom, for example, is not Bottom or Pyramus, but Bottom "in Pyramus," the one doing violence to the fiction of the other (151). Bottom's transformation into an ass's head earlier provides a literal metamorphosis; his meeting with Titania comes in the middle of the dream. "Titania and he are fancy against fact, not beauty and the beast" (155), but not even her magic can fully transpose Bottom into something that he essentially is not (3.1.123–24). He remains completely himself, even in the arms of the fairy queen (157).

In a forthcoming study, Patricia Parker has demonstrated the significance of Peter Quince's name. In legend, the quince fruit was regarded as a proper gift to newlyweds. She cites, for example, Alciato's *Book of Emblems* (1550), Emblem 204, which shows a quince tree loaded with fruit being gathered by a winged creature. The inscription below reads (translated from the Latin): "Solon of ancient times is said to have decided that Cydonian apples [i.e., quince] should be presented to newlyweds. Since they are pleasant to the taste and the digestion, their delicious charm stays in the mouth, so that the breath is made sweet by them." She also cites the emblem from Peacham's book of emblems, which shows a picture of a married man, a yoke on his shoulders and stocks locking his legs, with a quince in his upraised right hand. The inscriptions says,

> The stocks doe shew, his want of libertie,
> Not as he woont, to wander where he list:
> The yoke's an ensine of servilitie:
> The fruitfulness, the *Quince* within his fist,
>   Of wedlock tells, which *SOLON* did present,
>   T'*Athenian* Brides, the day to Church they went.

Quince and the associations his name invokes are thus appropriate for a wedding play and may suggest a further reason for Theseus's choice of "Pyramus and Thisbe," Quince's gift to the newly wedded couples.[43]

In his *A Theater of Envy* (1991) René Girard includes several chapters on *A Midsummer Night's Dream*, all of which are worth reading. One chapter focuses on the ritual of sacrifice in the play: "Sweet Puck!: Sacrifical Resolution in *A Midsummer Night's Dream*."[44] As Girard notes, no ones dies in a comedy, according to the rules of the genre, but this does not mean that violence or the threat of death must be absent. In his analysis of the end of 3.2, where Lysander and Demetrius chase each other about in the fog trying to kill one another, Puck subsitutes for each one and in effect becomes a surrogate victim, or sacrifice. As a scapegoat, he performs the typical function of providing "a single common target to the violence generated by human interaction," thus saving the community from that violence (236).

Puck is classically mythical, according to Girard. He is responsible for the initial confusion of the lovers by his errors and then for their reconciliation, not just because he puts the antidote to love-in-idleness on the right eyes, but more significantly because he saves Demetrius and Lysander from killing each other. Girard concludes that *A Midsummer Night's Dream* is "a stupendous treatise on the true nature of mythology."

> Through a reversal of the true perspective already implicit in the initial scapegoat transference, the reconciled doubles attribute their reconciliation not to the mimetic effect to which they really owe it and which they do not even perceive, but to the very victim whom they transfigure into a being capable of saving them as well as harming them. This is the genesis of the midsummer night fairies; the account of the night that the lovers render to Theseus and Hippolyta is distorted in the strict mythological sense. All mimetic desire has vanished and, in its stead, we have the dual action of Puck, first as troublemaker and then as a savior. (236)

Of course, *A Midsummer Night's Dream* is not a treatise; it is a dramatic comedy, doubtless Shakespeare's first triumph in the genre. But affinities with, or uses of, myth and ritual can clearly be seen, thanks to these and other critics who work in this critical mode.[45]

NOTES

1. Norman N. Holland, *Psychoanalysis and Shakespeare*. New York: McGraw-Hill, 1966, 69–70. Holland adds that such an interpretation would apply to the transpositions of the lovers, too, and to dreams, thus giving a richer significance to the play's title.

2. Ibid.

3. Ibid. Holland cites Freud and Breuer, *Studies in Hysteria* (1893–1995), ch. 3, and *The Standard Edition of the Complete Psychological Works of Sigmund Freud*, trans. James Strachey et al. 24 vols. London: Hogarth Press, 1940–42, 2: 250–51.

4. Holland, *Psychoanalysis and Shakespeare*, 106. He cites Jack Lindsay, "Shakespeare and Tom Thumb," *Life and Letters* 58 (1948), 119–27.

5. Weston A. Gui, "Bottom's Dream," *American Imago* 9 (1952–53), 251–305; cited and summarized by Holland, *Psychoanalysis and Shakespeare*, 243–44.

6. Donald F. Jacobson, "A Note on Shakespeare's *A Midsummer Night's Dream*," *American Imago* 19 (1962), 21–26; cited and summarized by Holland, *Psychoanalysis and Shakespeare*, 244–45.

7. Morton Kaplan, "*The American Imago* in Retrospect: An Article-Review," *Literature and Psychology* 13 (1963), 112–16.

8. Holland, *Psychoanalysis and Shakespeare*, 245.

9. Alex Aronson, *Psyche and Symbol in Shakespeare*. Bloomington: Indiana University Press, 1972, 204–5.

10. Ibid., 106. Aronson cites C. G. Jung, *Collected Works*, trans. R.F.C. Hull. New York: Pantheon, 1953–67, 9, 1: 263/472.

11. Aronson, *Psyche and Symbol*, 328, n. 8.

12. Norman N. Holland, "Hermia's Dream," in *Representing Shakespeare*, ed. Murray M. Schwartz and Coppélia Kahn, 1. Baltimore: Johns Hopkins University Press, 1980.

13. Holland (ibid.) cites Marjorie Garber, *Dream in Shakespeare*. New Haven, Conn.: Yale University Press, 1974, 72–74; and Melvin D. Faber, "Hermia's Dream: Royal Road to *A Midsummer Night's Dream*," *Literature and Psychology* 22 (1972), 179–90.

14. On the relationship between feminist criticism and psychoanalytic approaches, see Madelon Gohlke, " 'I Wooed Thee with My Sword': Shakespeare's Tragic Paradigm," in *Representing Shakespeare*, ed. Murray M. Schwartz and Coppélia Kahn, 170–87. Baltimore: Johns Hopkins University Press, 1980.

15. See Juliet Dusinberre, *Shakespeare and the Nature of Women*. 2d ed. New York: St. Martin's Press, 1996, xvii. Dusinberre's preface to the second edition, published twenty years after the first, surveys the development of gender criticism, especially but not exclusively in relation to Shakespeare studies.

16. In later comedies, beginning with Portia in *The Merchant of Venice*, Shakespeare's comic heroines show even greater strength of character as well as great resourcefulness. See Linda Bamber, *Comic Women, Tragic Men: A Study of Gender and Genre in Shakespeare*. Stanford, Calif.: Stanford University Press, 1982.

17. *The Woman's Part: Feminist Criticism of Shakespeare*, ed. Carolyn Ruth Swift Lenz, Gayle Greene, and Carol Thomas Neely. Urbana: University of Illinois Press, 1980, 3. Madelon Gohlke's essay, cited in note 14, first appeared in this anthology.

18. Shirley Nelson Garner, "*A Midsummer Night's Dream*: 'Jack Shall Have Jill; / Naught Shall Go Ill,' " *Women's Studies* 9 (1981), 47–63; reprinted in *"A Midsummer Night's Dream": Critical Essays*, ed. Dorothea Kehler, 127–43. New York: Garland, 1998. References are to the reprint.

19. Helen Hackett, *William Shakespeare: "A Midsummer Night's Dream."* Plymouth, England: Northcote House, 1997, 17–31.

20. Christy Desmet, "Disfiguring Women with Masculine Tropes: A Rhetorical Reading of *A Midsummer Night's Dream*," in *"A Midsummer Night's Dream": Critical Essays*, ed. Dorothea Kehler, 310. New York: Garland, 1998.

21. In *Erotic Politics: Desire on the Renaissance Stage*, ed. Susan Zimmerman, 157. New York: Routledge, 1992.

22. Terence Hawkes, *William Shakespeare: "King Lear."* Plymouth, England: Northcote House, 1995, 11.

23. In *Rewriting the Renaissance: The Discourses of Sexual Difference in Early Modern Europe*, ed. Margaret W. Ferguson, Maureen Quilligan, and Nancy J. Vickers, 65–87. Chicago: University of Chicago Press, 1986. A longer and more extensively documented version of the essay first appeared in *Representations* (Spring 1983), 61–94.

24. In Kehler, *Critical Essays*, 145–61; originally published in *Renaissance Papers 1986*, ed. Dale B. J. Randall and Joseph Porter, 11–30. Durham, N.C.: Southeastern Renaissance Conference, 19860. References are to Kehler's reprint.

25. Walter Cohen, "The Artisan Theatres of Renaissance England and Spain," *Theatre Journal* 35 (1983), 516.

26. See also Marcia McDonald, "Bottom's Space: Historicizing Comic Theory and Practice in *A Midsummer Night's Dream*," in *Acting Funny: Comic Theory and Practice in Shakespeare's Plays*, ed. Frances Teague, 85–108. Rutherford, N.J.: Fairleigh Dickinson Press, 1994. McDonald puts the staging of "Pyramus and Thisbe" in the context of the theatrical controversy of the period and focuses on Bottom's important role.

> Shakespeare's creation of a play script that allows a socially marginal, politically threatening figure to create a powerful theatrical experience not sanctioned by any authoritative voice in Elizabethan England puts his theater squarely in the debate over the function of the stage. . . . *A Midsummer Night's Dream* takes all the charges of scurrility, vice, sedition, lasciviousness, and social disorder, and all the strategies of stage type, comic representation, and audience response, producing through its metatheatricality a construcion of theater that expands the theater's power to reproduce and revise the language and codes of its culture. (102)

27. Hawkes, *William Shakespeare*, 15, citing Jonathan Dollimore, "Critical Developments: Cultural Materialism, Feminism and Gender Critique, and New Historicism," in *Shakespeare: A Bibliographical Guide*, ed. Stanley Wells, 414. Oxford: Oxford University Press, 1990.

28. In *New Casebooks: "A Midsummer Night's Dream,"* ed. Richard Dutton. New York: St. Martin's Press, 1996, 223–58.

29. In 1914 "Nedar" made an appearance on stage in Harley Granville Barker's production, but it was as Helena's father, not her mother. Hawkes, *William Shakespeare*, 247–48.

30. In *From the Bard to Broadway*, ed. Karelisa V. Hartigan. Lanham, Md.: University Press of America, 1987, 191–212.

31. In Margo Hendricks, "Obscured by Dreams: Race, Empire, and Shakespeare's *A Midsummer Night's Dream*," *Shakespeare Quarterly* 47 (1996), 37–60.

32. Hendricks considers the possibility that the Indian boy may be the product of human and fairy mixedness (ibid., 56).

33. Northrop Frye, *Anatomy of Criticism*. Princeton, N.J.: Princeton University Press, 1957, 136.

34. See A. C. Hamilton, *Northrop Frye: Anatomy of His Criticism*. Toronto: University of Toronto Press, 1990, 136.

35. Frye, *Anatomy*, 163.

36. Hamilton, *Northrop Frye*, 136.

37. Northrop Frye, *A Natural Perspective*. New York: Columbia University Press, 1965, 141.

38. Ibid., 118.

39. Hamilton, *Northrop Frye*, 137.

40. Frye, *Anatomy*, 182.

41. Ibid., 183; Hamilton, *Northrop Frye*, 138.

42. C. L. Barber, *Shakspeare's Festive Comedy: A Study of Dramatic Form and Its Relation to Social Custom*. Princeton, N.J.: Princeton University Press, 1959, 4.

43. The information in this paragraph is based on Professor Parker's paper delivered at the biannual International Shakespeare Conference held in Stratford-upon-Avon, England, in August 2002. A version of her paper will appear in *Shakespeare Survey* in 2003.

44. René Girard, *Theater of Envy: William Shakespeare*. New York: Oxford University Press, 1991, 234–42.

45. See, for example, Edward Berry, *Shakespeare's Comic Rites*. Cambridge, England: Cambridge University Press, 1984, which focuses on the rites of passage in the comedies.

6

THE PLAY IN PERFORMANCE

Where and when *A Midsummer Night's Dream* was first publicly performed is not known. The Globe theater was not yet built; it probably was not performed at The Theatre, where James Burbage was having problems with his lease for the land. The play was in the repertoire of the Lord Chamberlain's Men (later, the King's Men) for many years, if we can credit the title page of the 1600 quarto, which claims that the play was "sundry times publikely acted." Gary Williams has suggested that it might be the "play of Robin goode-fellow" performed before King James, possibly at Hampton Court, in January 1604.[1] Edward Sharpham's *The Fleire* (1607) may allude to Shakespeare's play, which William Jaggard included among the Pavier quartos in 1619 before he became involved with the Folio collection. According to Williams, John Taylor, the Water-poet, may be remembering the play in performance when he wrote in the foreword to *Sir Gregory Nonsense* (1622), "I say, as it is applausefully written, and commended to posterity, in the Midsummer-Night's Dream, If we offend, it is with our good will, we came with no intent but to offend, and show our simple skill."[2]

A Midsummer Night's Dream is among the four plays listed as performed by the King's Men at Hampton Court on October 17, 1630, probably in the great hall.[3] E. K. Chambers claimed that the play was presented on a Sunday before the Bishop of Lincoln, John Williams, and his guests at Buckden Palace, near Huntingdon. The host was fined for violating the Sabbath, and the principal player was punished by being placed in the stocks wearing an ass's head with a bundle of hay at his feet.[4] Other allusions or references suggest the play's popularity in the early seventeenth century, before public playing was discontinued in 1642, when the Puritans, now in full control of the government, dismantled all the theaters.

The original performances in the public theater took full advantage of the thrust stage, which brought the actors and audience into close proximity with each other. Unlike modern theaters, the stage had little, if any, scenery; hence, the emphasis was placed on the language as spoken, or rather declaimed, by the actors, not on spectacle, the least important aspect of dramatic performance, according to Aristotle's *Poetics*. With no obviously starring roles, ensemble acting and doubling of parts were almost certainly featured, although Will Kempe most likely played the virtuoso role of Bottom and Burbage played Oberon, perhaps doubled with Theseus.[5] Audiences stood around the apron stage exposed to the weather or, if they paid another penny for admission, sat in the galleries that surrounded the stage. A few exceptional members of the audience might be seated in the "lord's room" above the stage, or on the stage itself. Performances were held in daylight with no artificial lighting required, until the King's Men began using their "private" indoor theater, the Blackfriars Theatre, in 1609.

The stage was entered from the tiring house (the area behind the stage where actors dressed and awaited their cues), usually from one of two doors. Both are noted in the Folio stage directions at the beginning of act 2, although it is possible that Puck occasionally sprang to the stage from a trap door beneath.[6] Action was continuous in the public playhouses with no intervals, but the Folio direction at the end of 3.1, "They sleepe all the Act," indicates that when the play was later adapted for private theater, intervals were instituted.[7] Although scenery was sparse, preset throne chairs for Theseus and Hippolyta might have been used to establish the court setting in 1.1,[8] although they are by no means essential. The forest scenes might have been suggested by having the First Fairy, on entering at 2.1, hang a few boughs of greenery on the pillars that held up the canopy over the stage, and possibly some sort of apparatus was used for Titania's bower in 2.2 or the hawthorn brake in 3.1.[9]

Costumes could be and often were elaborate. The finery worn by Theseus and Hippolyta as the Duke and Duchess of Athens was Elizabethan with perhaps some classical embellishments. Oberon and Titania, as their counterparts in the forest world, dressed similarly. Ronald Watkins and Jeremy Lemmon believe that Puck was dressed as a king's jester, complete with coxcomb and motley (25), but the more traditional costume of the English sprite—as he appears, for example, in Ben Jonson's masque *Love Restored* (1616)—fits the character much better.[10] The fairies were not gauzy ballet dancers dressed in tutus with wings attached to them, as later represented in art and performance, and they were not female.[11] Bottom refers to one as "Monsieur Cobweb," another as "Monsieur Mustardseed," and a third as "Cavalery [i.e., Cavalier] Peaseblossom" (4.1.8–22). Williams believes the little Indian boy, dressed appropriately, was likely present onstage in 2.1, although he is not mentioned in the stage directions (1997, 24). Cutting through two levels—the mythical-historical and the supernatural—was the downright realistic. The rude mechanicals, or "hard-handed workmen of Athens," looked just like their derivatives as Warwickshire craftsmen, all dressed as we should expect in Shakespeare's time.

The young lovers were also dressed in Elizabethan fashion, not quite so elaborately as Theseus and Hippolyta, but similarly embellished.[12] The men carried swords, as required by their attempted duel (3.2.401–12). Few other props were necessary, though of course Bottom needed his removable ass's head, and for the play-within-the-play, Starveling as Moonshine needed his lantern, bush, and dog (5.1.242–44). A lion's costume for Snug and some kind of wall paraphernalia for Snout were also needed for "Pyramus and Thisbe." Musicians sitting in the gallery directly above the stage supplied the music for the songs and dances.[13]

LATER SEVENTEENTH- AND EIGHTEENTH-CENTURY PRODUCTIONS OF *DREAM*

"For almost two hundred years, from 1642 to 1840, *A Midsummer Night's Dream* was never seen in its entirety in the English or continental theatre" (Williams 1997, 38). What were seen were various adaptations, including a "droll," or short comic piece, a Purcell opera, and other versions. One droll, called *Bottom the Weaver*, published in 1661, maintains on its title page, "It hath been often publickely Acted by some of his Majesties Comedians, and lately, privately, presented, by several Apprentices for their harmless recreation, with Great Applause."[14] The droll, which centers upon Bottom and his friends, preserves all their episodes taken from the text of the Second Folio (1632), but it omits the young lovers, and the roles of Titania, Oberon, and Puck are severely cut. A few brief additions, based on Shakespeare's lines, are included to provide continuity. The printed list of actors indicates that a number of parts may have been doubled, especially the roles of Theseus and Oberon, and may reflect an earlier stage tradition (Halio 1994, 14). Similar adaptations had long since been known on the Continent, thanks to English strolling players, especially in Germany, since the comedy of the mechanicals was close to that of the peasant comic tradition of Hans Sachs (Williams 1997, 39–40).

The reason for the adaptations in England that separated the "Pyramus and Thisbe" plot from the rest of the action doubtless has much to do with notions of dramatic decorum in the late seventeenth and early eighteenth centuries. By 1660, when the theaters reopened in London after the restoration of the monarchy under Charles II, English drama was heavily influenced by the neoclassical doctrines imported from France, where the court had resided in exile during the Commonwealth period. The reaction of Samuel Pepys to a performance he saw of *A Midsummer Night's Dream* in 1662 may reflect the taste of his time:

> Then to the King's Theatre, where we saw "Midsummer Night's Dream," which I had never seen before nor shall ever again, for it is the most insipid ridiculous play that I ever saw in my life. I saw, I confess, some good dancing and some handsome women, which was all my pleasure.[15]

By this time, of course, following the French lead, women had taken the female roles previously played by boys. Williams speculates that Pepys may have seen a musical version of the play (1997, 40), although there is plenty of music and dance in the original script. For the next thirty years, the play dropped out of the repertoire.

When the play reemerged, it did so spectacularly but utterly transmogrified. Under Continental influences, Elkanah Settle adapted Shakespeare's play as an opera called *The Fairy Queen* with music by Henry Purcell. Thomas Betterton produced it in 1692 at Dorset Gardens Theatre, where it was revived the next year with additional songs and music by Purcell. Purcell, however, did not score a single line of Shakespeare's text. The Shakespeare parts in this severely cut and mangled version were all spoken and acted. The lovers, the fairies, the rude mechanicals are all there, but so are a number of new characters: Coridon, Mopsa, nymphs, and "a Chorus of *Fawns*, and *Naids*, with *Woodmen*, and *Haymakers* Dancers." In addition, allegorical figures—Night, Mystery, Secrecy, Sleep—and their attendants appear, as well as Spring, Summer, Autumn, and Winter with Phoebus for a "Dance of the Four Seasons." The opera had still more for the delight of the age: Juno, a chorus of

Chinese men and women, a dance of six monkeys, and "a Grand Dance of 24 *Chinese*," as recorded in "The Names of the Persons" in Jacob Tonson's edition of 1692.[16]

The Glorious Revolution of 1689 had brought William of Orange and his queen, Mary, to the English throne. According to Williams, *The Fairy Queen*, as adapted by Settle and Purcell, was a tribute to the royal couple, "an allegory on marital harmony," the model for which was found in William and Mary's marriage (1997, 44). All references to Athens were eliminated, and Hippolyta's role disappeared entirely. Theseus is called simply "the Duke." The thorough "Englishing" of the play probably was an attempt to to provide a greater homogeneity by avoiding the mixing of Greeks, Gothic fairy mythology, and Elizabethan workmen in keeping with a neoclassical sense of unity.[17] Here and throughout the next century, attempts were made to regularize and "modernize" Shakespeare's language and verse. In the process, about half of Shakespeare's lines were cut from *A Midsummer Night's Dream*.

Aided by advances in theatrical machinery and movable stage sets, spectacle became increasingly important on the Restoration stage, as it has done subsequently (witness our lavish contemporary musicals, for example). *The Fairy Queen* was "second to none for mechanical marvels."[18] At the end of act 3, for example, Titania orders her elves to prepare a "Fairy Mask," to entertain Bottom, and at once her bower becomes an "Enchanted Lake." Greater spectacle came at the ending of the opera, when Oberon and Titania show the wedded couples and their assembled guests Juno "*in a Machine drawn by Peacocks.*" "*While a Symphony Plays, the Machine moves forward, and the Peacocks spread their Tails, and fill the middle of the Theater*"; Juno then sings a song to the lovers. As Oberon and the others depart, a symphony plays, and the scene is suddenly illuminated, revealing a Chinese garden, where a Chinese man and woman sing, six monkeys come from between the trees and dance, and two sopranos sing "in parts" a song summoning the god Hymen, who appears and responds with a song of his own. The Chinese man and woman dance, then all the dancers join in after "The Grand Chorus" (Halio 1994, 17). This is not quite the conclusion, but it is enough to indicate the utterly un-Shakespearean kind of spectacle the audience loved.

Settle and Purcell's opera directly influenced productions of Shakespeare's *Dream* in the next century. In David Garrick's and George Colman's adaptations, the text was interspersed with songs and dances as well as spectacle, which appealed to audiences more than "straight" productions would have done. The first of these adaptations was *The Fairies* (1755), an opera written by Garrick and a pupil of George Frideric Handel, John Christopher Smith, with songs from Shakespeare, John Milton, Edmund Waller, John Dryden, and other poets.[19] The courtiers, lovers, and fairies were retained, but the mechnicals were not. Though listed among the dramatis personae, Hippolyta had no lines, and speeches by other characters were sharply curtailed to make room for the songs. Unlike in Purcell's opera, however, some of Shakespeare's verse was set to music (for example, Helena's lines, "O happy fair," 1.1.182–84). In all, twenty-one songs, as well as several dances, were interspersed throughout the dialogue, including some songs from *Much Ado about Nothing* and *The Tempest*. According to Williams, "The work is a slight pastoral pastiche of a few elements of the plots of Shakespeare's moon-crossed lovers and the quarrel between Oberon and Titania" (1997, 67). Only a quarter of Shakespeare's lines remained in the text; the omissions were explained in an advertisement in the 1755 edition: "It was feared that even the best poetry would appear tedious when only supported by Recitative." Most of act 5 was cut, including the play-within-the-play. Instead of Shakespeare's fairy masque at the end, Theseus summoned the couples to the altar, and a chorus sang "Hail to love, and welcome joy!" (Halio 1994, 18–19).

In 1763 Garrick, actually a staunch admirer of Shakespeare, attempted to stage something closer to the original text of *A Midsummer Night's Dream*, but his efforts to do so were effectively hindered by his colleague, George Colman, and the result was a fiasco. Since Garrick was then living abroad, Colman supervised the rehearsals and altered Garrick's script considerably, cutting an additional 561 lines originally retained by Garrick. Colman also added lines, eighteen for example at the end of 1.2, which turned the first meeting of Quince & Co. into what G. W. Stone has called "a glee club rehearsal."[20] "Pyramus and Thisbe" was entirely omitted from the last act. This version, which met with terrible reviews, lasted only one night in performance. Three days later, Colman attempted to recoup some of his losses and produced *A Fairy Tale* as an afterpiece to his *Jealous Wife*. Unlike *The Fairies*, this two-act skit of 400 lines and thirteen songs includes the Athenian workmen and the fairies but omits all the lovers and courtiers. Bottom is not transformed into an ass's head; thunder and lightning scare off his friends, leaving Bottom to be discovered and wooed by Titania. This business continues much as in the *Dream*, but very abbreviated, as Titania and Oberon become reconciled, Puck removes a sound-asleep Bottom from the stage, an air is sung about Orpheus, and a lark heralds daybreak and the end of the play.

Colman's afterpiece became very popular, with many performances between 1763 and 1766 and one in 1767.[21] It was revived for the last time in 1777, but the seven performances given that summer were the last of the eighteenth-century adaptations and revivals.[22] No other adaptations took the boards until Frederick Reynold's operatic version for John Philip Kemble in 1816, which held the stage in some form or other for many years.

THE NINETEENTH CENTURY

Nineteenth-century productions of Shakespeare's plays are best remembered for their lavish scenic displays and the corresponding attempts made at historical authenticity. As theater technology advanced, so did elaborate stagings of the plays. Scene painting surpassed anything previously seen, and Felix Mendelssohn's overture (1826) and incidental music (1843) to *A Midsummer Night's Dream* had a powerful impact on productions. Garrick's attempts to restore at least some of Shakespeare's texts gathered momentum and eventually drove such redactions as Nahum Tate's *King Lear* from the boards. At the same time, Romantic criticism, which tended to emphasize the beauty of Shakespeare's conceptions as well as his poetry, insisted that the plays could never be as well realized in performance as they could be in the "theater of the imagination." This was especially true of Shakespeare's most imaginative comedy, these critics proclaimed. Writing about the first performance of Reynolds's production at Covent Garden, William Hazlitt said, "All that is fine in the play was lost in the representation."[23]

Reynolds's production was an adaptation of Shakespeare's comedy, not the thing itself, but spectacle (which Hazlitt commended as its only excellence) had again triumphed over poetry, and "improvements" on Shakespeare continued to corrupt the text. Interspersed among Shakespeare's lines were new speeches and songs as well as alterations of the original language, and a whole new scene and part of another were added. Transpositions of scenes can also be detected in the script: "Pyramus and Thisbe" was enacted earlier, and the productions ended with the discovery and awakening of the couples in the forest, an air by Hermia, and a rousing recitative, "Warriors! March on!"; whereupon, instead of Shakespeare's fairy masque and Puck's epilogue, a dozen or more soldiers entered in procession on their way to the Hall of State in a grand pageant proclaiming Theseus's triumphs. No wonder Hazlitt reacted as he did.[24]

Spectacle and operatic adaptation thus continued to overwhelm Shakespeare's fairy play, although as George Odell admits, they must have presented "very pretty pictures" (1920, 2: 113), as attractive in their way as the designs for *The Fairy Queen* must have been earlier. By 1833, however, Reynolds's adaptation had dwindled to an afterpiece of only two acts, whose only distinction is that it was the first to use Mendelssohn's great overture.[25] Not until the end of the nineteenth century, which saw the experiments of William Poel and Harley Granville Barker, did reaction against extravagant display begin in earnest. Meanwhile, the most important productions of the *Dream* during the century are those of Madame Vestris at Covent Garden in 1840, Samuel Phelps at Sadler's Wells in 1853, and Charles Kean at the Princess Theatre in 1856.

Although the Italian contralto and theatrical manager Lucia Elizabeth Vestris did much to restore some of Shakespeare's language to *A Midsummer Night's Dream*, her production nevertheless continued the tradition begun a century and a half earlier of introducing spectacle and additional songs and dances. Setting a precedent by enacting Oberon herself, Vestris kept more of Shakespeare's major passages, such as Titania's "forgeries of jealousy" speech (2.1.81–117), than her predecessors had done. Although mid-Victorian decorum dictated certain cuts—for example, the reference to "big-bellied sails" and "wanton wind" (2.1.128–29, 131)—Hermia still spoke of giving up her "virgin patent" (1.1.80), and at the end Theseus twice summons the lovers to bed (5.1.342, 345). In later productions these would change to "maiden heart" and "Lovers, away."[26]

Vestris's colleague, James Robinson Planché, deserves much of the credit for such integrity as the script retained of Shakespeare's original.[27] He was also the scenic and costume supervisor and devised the elegant staging of the last scene, which he developed from a reading of Shakespeare's lines rather than by disregarding them. It was nonetheless spectacular, with more than fifty fairies flying or dancing through architectural galleries, up and down palace stairs, carrying blue and yellow lanterns (Griffiths 1979, 394). Vestris used music to set off Shakespeare's words, not to replace them, and to develop a dramatic purpose. The fourteen songs, taken from Shakespeare's text, were sung by fairies to distinguish them further from the mortals. Mendelssohn's overture raised the curtain, as it had for Ludwig Tieck's production in Berlin thirteen years earlier (Salgado 1975, 118). Thereafter, Vestris stayed with one composer, Thomas Simpson Cooke, instead of a variety of composers, as her predecessors had done.[28]

Costumes in Vestris's production were classical for the Athenians, sandals and tunics for the mechanicals, and variations on Greek themes for the winged fairies (Griffiths 1979, 392). Williams explains Vestris's decision to play Oberon as an attempt to capitalize on her sexual appeal as well as her musical talent (1997, 93, 96). A woman as the fairy king, moreover, would have addressed patriarchal Victorian culture in a variety of ways. A woman, Queen Victoria, was once again on the British throne, but perhaps more important, a woman in the role of fairy king could better emphasize the ethereal quality associated with such beings. In any event, with only one exception, women played the role of Oberon in every major English and American production of the *Dream* until 1914 (93). Puck was also played by a woman in Vestris's production, and in her first appearance she rose up center stage sitting on a mushroom, a delightful alteration of the script that Charles Kean also used when eight-year-old Ellen Terry performed the role in his production a few years later. Although we do not see a woman as Oberon today, it is not uncommon for an actress to play Puck in modern productions.[29]

The Tieck-Mendelssohn production of 1843 was the first time the full-scale *A Midsummer Night's Dream*, which became a favorite of German and Austrian audiences, appeared on the German stage.[30] Commissioned by the king of Prussia, it premiered in Potsdam's court theater, using Mendelssohn's incidental music and August Wilhelm von Schlegel's translation of 1798. Shakespeare in translation was already popular in Germany, both on the page and on the stage. Tieck was very interested in Elizabethan staging, and in 1836 he had built a replica of the Fortune Theatre with the help of architect Gottfried Semper. His staging of the *Dream*, which had to use the proscenium arch of the Potsdam theater, was a compromise between the Elizabethan and the nineteenth-century pictorial stages. The costumes were a mix of Greek, old German, and sixteenth-century Spanish designs. A full orchestra, used to play Mendelssohn's score, filled the pit in front of the stage. Because Mendelssohn and Tieck had not coordinated their work on the music and the text, some discrepancies resulted, not all of which could be fully reconciled in the production. Among the most well-known elements of Mendelssohn's score are the fairy march for the entrance of Oberon and Titania and their trains in act 2 and, of course, the famous "Wedding March," used for the court's exit at the end of act 5, which lasted a full five minutes. It celebrated Theseus as "a beneficent Elizabethan Greek hero, with Prussian overtones," a tribute in its way to King Friedrich, who had commissioned the production (Williams 1997, 108). The production itself was a tribute to and a validation of German culture, which had by this time claimed Shakespeare as her own.

A decade later in London, Samuel Phelps produced *A Midsummer Night's Dream* emphasizing its ethereal, dreamlike quality. Even critic Henry Morley, who believed this play above all others was "unactable," recognized Phelps's accomplishment (Halio 1994, 25). "There is no ordinary scene-shifting," Morley wrote, "but, as in dreams, one scene is made to glide insensibly into another."[31] To achieve this effect, Phelps's scene designer, Frederick Fenton, used the newly installed gas lighting, a diorama, and a piece of greenish-blue gauze let down in front of the stage for the forest scenes.[32] Phelps himself played Bottom and used a young but well-trained cast of actors dressed appropriately to blend in with the overall scenic effect. Music there was and dancing, but not the songs from Vestris's production. The musical score has not been found; the 1861 revival used Mendelssohn's music as arranged by W. H. Montgomery.[33]

By mid-century Mendelssohn's music—both the overture and the incidental music—was becoming a fixture in many stage productions of the *Dream*. In 1854 two New York productions, one by William Evans Burton and the other by Thomas Berry and E. A. Marshall, advertised the whole of Mendelssohn's score in their stagings. Burton erroneously claimed that it was used in his production for the first time anywhere. These were not the first American productions of the play. An operatic version was staged in 1826; and in 1841, possibly inspired by Vestris's success, Charlotte Cushman played Oberon in a nonoperatic version.[34] The competing New York productions of 1854 were probably inspired by Phelps's triumph, although Burton claimed he had never seen the play staged. He insisted that the stage business and scenic effects were all original and the costumes were historically correct. In act 2, Oberon and Titania descended in aerial cars, and in act 4 mists rose at sunrise from the valleys and the sun beamed powerfully (Shattuck 1976, 113). This was an age, we must remember, that stressed archeological verisimilitude, as in Charles Kean's spectacular productions. Barry's production was less successful. Nevertheless, Shakespeare was coming of age on the American stage, although still following British leads.

To keep performances in 1856 under three hours' duration, allowing time for music, dance, and cumbersome scene shifts, Charles Kean's production at the Princess Theatre of *A Midsummer Night's Dream* cut

Costume designs (Titania and her fairies) for Charles Kean's production (1856). By permission of the Folger Shakespeare Library.

more than 800 lines from Shakespeare's text. In addition to Mendelssohn's music, the work of other composers was used. A woman, Fanny Ternan, played Oberon, and the fairies were all played by adults. Morley praised the production but criticized some innovations. He especially objected to the maypole ballet that ended act 3, which replaced the quarrel between Hermia and Helena. He described the fairies as "not airy beings of the colour of the greenwood, or of the sky, or robed in misty white, but glittering in the most brilliant dresses, with a crust of bullion about their legs" (Morley 1891, 134). Still, the dance earned an encore, displaying the "depraved taste" of the audience, according to Morley.

Although Kean eschewed exact historical authenticity, setting the play in the Age of Pericles rather than the mythical time of Theseus, his set designs won high praise. The gorgeous scenery detracted from the poetry, stated Morley, who liked the sets (1891, 133). In 1.1, instead of an unspecified room in Theseus's palace, an elaborate painted set filled the stage. Kean outdid all others, including Vestris, in his use of spectacle, using as many as ninety fairies tripping up and down the stairs of Theseus's palace in act 5 waving bell-like lanterns (see Halio 1994, 28).

Kean's production inspired Laura Keene's in New York in 1859, as well as several others.[35] It used both Kean's text (with still further cuts), the maypole ballet, and an opera singer, Fanny Stockton, as Oberon. Keene herself, a disciple of Vestris, played Puck. Despite its flaws, the production was revived in 1867, doubtless owing to its scenic splendor, with a different cast.[36]

THE TWENTIETH CENTURY

By the end of the nineteenth century, spectacle had become primary when staging Shakespeare's plays. This was especially true of the celebrated productions of Augustin Daly and Herbert Beerbohm Tree, the most popular ones of their period. Daly staged the play several times, beginning in 1873, with "the famous Golden Quartette of California, in the dress of Satyrs," singing the lullaby to Titania in act 2.[37] In his 1888 revival, Isadora Duncan in papier-maché wings, was one of the dancing fairies, who had electric lights powered by portable batteries fitted to their costumes to provide glimmering effects. George Bernard Shaw reviewed this production at Daly's Theatre with harsh criticism for Daly's illusionism and for casting a woman as Oberon, although he praised Ada Rehan's Helena.[38] In January 1900, Tree produced his *Dream* at Her Majesty's Theatre in London with even more elaborate scenery and effects. It rivaled all previous productions, according to contemporary accounts, such as that given in *The Atheneum* on January 20: "No spectacle equally artistic has been seen on the English stage. The glades near Athens in which the action passes are the perfection of sylvan loveliness, the palace of Theseus is a marvel of scenic illusion."[39] Mendelssohn's music was used, and the fairies, "ebullitions of mirth and joyousness," received special praise. Tree even went so far as to introduce live rabbits running across the stage.[40] More than 200,000 people came to see this splendiforous production.[41]

Although in productions of *A Midsummer Night's Dream* spectacle and illusionism continued well into the twentieth century,[42] the winds of change were blowing. While some may have belittled William Poel's attempts in "Elizabethan" stagings of *A Midsummer Night's Dream* and other plays (Williams 1997, 125), the reaction against spectacle had begun to set in. Chief among those who tried new ways of producing Shakespeare's plays was Harley Granville Barker, whose staging of the *Dream* in 1914 followed productions of *The Winter's Tale* and *Twelfth Night*, in which he aimed to restore the intimacy between actors and audience he believed was a characteristic of Shakespeare's playhouse experiences. He adapted the proscenium stage, which was now standard in British theaters, to accommodate an apron or thrust stage, as used in Elizabethan playhouses. Instead of the footlights that cast long shadows of the actors, he used spotlights mounted on the front rail of the dress circle, which brought a more "democratic light, falling equally on principals and supers."[43] Barker eschewed realistic settings, preferring impressionistic designs and using draped curtains to this end. Verse speaking was "swift, melodic and natural," with very few cuts in the text.[44] His greatest innovation was his use of gilded fairies, enacted by full-sized adults (men for Oberon's train, women for Titania's). These were introduced instead of the gauzy, bewinged children who had become commonplace in productions, though Barker later came to have second thoughts about this innovation. To emphasize the fairies' supernatural quality, Barker directed them to walk in a stiff, dignified gait, covered as they were with gold paint and in places actual gold leaf.[45] Mendelssohn's score was replaced by Cecil Sharp's English folk music.

In the view of some critics, Barker's experiments were only partly successful. He was still ahead of his time, at least in the Anglo-American theater world. His influence was greater on the European Continent, especially Germany, where directors like Max Reinhardt were also replacing realism with impressionism. Reinhardt's productions of the *Dream*, which became popular all over Europe, culminated in his staging of the play in Hollywood, California, in 1935 and later his motion picture made with William Dieterle, starring Mickey Rooney as Puck, Anita Louise as Titania, Victor Jory as Oberon, and James Cagney as Bottom. Reinhardt, who preferred a light, airy style, retained all of Shakespeare's text, though in translation (except, of course, in America). He kept Mendelssohn's overture and incidental music—how could he not in Germany?

Reinhardt's productions were by no means static but evolved over time from a mixture of illusionism and impressionism to a more suggestive, symbolist treatment of light and shade. For example, green curtains were dropped before a practically bare stage to suggest the forest. A new sense of play infused the production, and the physicality of the lovers, including their sexual impulses, was apparent. In Salzburg, Austria, and later in Oxford, England, Reinhardt moved the production outdoors, but not to any of the college gardens, where the play is often performed today. Instead, he preferred the great meadow at South Park, Headington Hill, which gave the impression of "limitless space," or so he believed.[46] At the Hollywood Bowl in 1935 he risked starting a forest fire (it did not happen) when he ordered a torchlight procession to descend from the Hollywood Hills for the grand wedding procession in act 5. The production was a huge success and encouraged him to go forward with the film version.

In England, experimental stagings and traditional ones continued to vie with each other, occasionally striking a compromise in productions such as those by William Bridges-Adams presented between the two world wars (Halio 1994, 39–40). The competition continues to this day, sometimes going to extremes. The farthest swing of the pendulum away from Shakespeare's text and toward spectacle and dance was a totally wordless *Dream* using Mendelssohn's music, choreographed by George Balanchine in 1962, and subsequently revived.[47]

One of the more interesting American experiments in staging the play was a lesser known production by Alex Reeves in 1958 at Howard Payne College, Texas, which toured England and was staged at the Cambridge Arts Theatre in the summer of 1959. Called a "Western style" production, its setting was changed from Athens to a Texas ranch in the 1880s. It opened with a rousing square dance, followed by Quince & Co. gathered around a campfire, speaking in an exaggerated Texas drawl. The male mortals wore Stetson hats, six-guns, and leather chaps: the women wore bustles and bows, except Hippolyta, who was now a Native American princess. The fairies were little American Indians, too, making the association with Hippolyta closer. Except for occasional yells of "Yippee!" and "Wahoo!" the text was as Shakespeare wrote it. It was a well-spoken production without the burlesquing that might have been expected of such a transformation, and it won the hearts of British as well as American audiences. Apart from everything else, the production showed how well Shakespeare's plays, especially his comedies, can lend themselves to various, even unusual, settings. When at the same time the integrity of the texts is preserved, everything may conspire to help audiences see and hear the plays afresh.[48]

PETER BROOK AND THE ROYAL SHAKESPEARE COMPANY

To be able to see and hear the play afresh was certainly Peter Brook's aim in his watershed production for the Royal Shakespeare Company in 1970. Searching for a conception that would bring *A Midsummer Night's Dream* newly alive, he made magic the key to his production—along

Alan Howard as Oberon and John Kane as Puck in Peter Brook's Royal Shakespeare Company production (1970). Courtesy of Photofest.

with celebration, a celebration of theater.[49] Utterly opposed to "museum Shakespeare" and other kinds of what he has called "deadly Shakespeare," he banished traditional settings and costumes. In their place, he and Sally Jacobs, his designer, devised a set that was simply a three-sided white box, rather like a squash court, and dressed the actors (except the mechanicals[50]) in colorful, loose, satin costumes—ideas derived from watching a Chinese circus.[51] Before rehearsals even began, Brook had the cast practicing juggling tricks and acrobatics. In an interview with Ralph Berry, he explained what all this meant for him and why he used it:

> What I'm interested to see is not the historical sense but the actual, what makes meaning for me. And it was through that channel that we eventually, for instance in the *Dream*, came to say: what does magic, what does fairy magic actually mean as a reality within the two hours that you're in the theatre? Not as a convention, but as something that still has a reality? Maybe with completely different forms. The word "fairy" suggests a lot of things: it suggests dead associations. Far behind, it also suggests very living values.[52]

The "living values" that Brook wanted to capture became the motive for using magic, as in a modern Chinese circus, and the basis for his production.

Brook cut very little from the text, for he believed that *A Midsummer Night's Dream* was one of Shakespeare's more polished works, "an absolutely perfect play" (Berry 1989, 148). From the first day of rehearsals, Brook emphasized the need "to enlarge and intensify the text's meaning," mainly by searching out the "associations, the lines, the correspondences" in the play.[53] For example, Helena's reference to love's ability to transpose things "base and vile" to "form and dignity" (1.1.232–33) introduces the idea of "transformation"—including that of physical appearance—from dream world to actual world, "of transfigurations wrought by force of the imagination" (Selbourne 1982, 5). Brook required the actors to search for the "real" in the characters and in their emotions, and to convey this reality in the dialogue. He knew when they drew from their experience correctly or not, but he could not discover the experience for them (101). That was up to the actors themselves. Hard work though it was, it paid off handsomely.

Brook fully realized that productions should evolve, not only in rehearsal, but also in performance. Alan Howard, who played both Theseus and Oberon, found in the course of two or three years of the play's run an "ever-greater sense of secret meanings" on many levels. These meanings came from him and "made vibrations pass through Theseus into Oberon and back again across the whole play. The play was at its best when the whole cast was at a point of high attunement" (Berry 1989, 148). It was this "high attunement," virtuoso ensemble acting, that Brook strived for, for only in that way could the audience share fully enough in the creative accomplishment.

To engage the audience as fully as possible, Brook had his actors, when not part of a scene, watch the action from the galleries above the walls of the squash court stage. Hence, the actors were never uninvolved. Though they could move about freely on the galleries, they could also interact in the same way as the theater audience, providing a further "surround" for the action and emphasizing the play *as* play (Loney 1974, 47). The props were likewise distinctive. The magic flower, love-in-idleness, for example, was a silver dish spinning on a rod. The forest trees were coiled wires dropped from above, encircling and entangling the lovers. Occasionally, the fairies descended from above on swings or trapezes. Titania's bower was a large, feathery hammock, which descended and ascended as appropriate. The problem of Bottom's ass's head was solved by making him simply become an ass (51). All he used was a pair of earmuffs, a black button nose, and clogs attached to his feet. His facial expressions were thus never obscured in performance.

The music was likewise very distinctive. Richard Peaslee's score, or "organized noise" as it was called, involved a guitarist, two percussionists, a trombonist, and a trumpet player. He also used a strange instrument called a Free-Kas for the weird sounds Brook wanted. Much of the music developed from rehearsals, although Peaslee added some new songs later during the world tour. Some passages traditionally sung were not set to music, while others were scored for the first time (Loney 1974, 68–71). The overall effect was startling at first, like everything else, but it succeeded in helping to achieve Brook's ultimate goal.

Stunningly original as Brook's production was, not everyone delighted in it. Citing Jan Kott's effort to desentimentalize the play, Benedict Nightingale thought Brook had sentimentalized it all over again "in a new, more insidious way. His manic decoration," he wrote, "has deprived it of suffering, fear, horror, and, apart from one moment, when Bottom's phallus is crudely mimed by the fairies, even of lust."[54] John Russell Brown also severely criticized Brook's accomplishments, mainly for playing against the text. At 3.1.174–78, for example, instead of bringing Bottom silently to Titania's bower, the fairies carry him off in triumphant celebration. He further objected to the doubling of Theseus and Hippolyta with Oberon and Titania, "as if the actors' task was to make what likeness exists between the pairs as obvious and inescapable as possible, and to minimise the very considerable differences."[55] The justice of these and other negative comments may be debated, as they have been for decades, but without question audiences all over the world entered joyously into the spirit of the production, much as Brook had hoped. If Brook occasionally played against the text, as Brown pointed out, he also found ambiguities within it that could be and were exploited, uncovering new depths. His success, moreover, may be calculated in part by the numerous imitations of the production the world over as well as by the reactions of directors at the Royal Shakespeare Company and elsewhere. In a kind of anxiety of influence, these directors have tried to find other ways to awaken audiences newly to the play.

At the Royal Shakespeare Company, or the RSC as it is familiarly called, John Barton in 1977, Ron Daniels in 1981, Bill Alexander in 1986, and Adrian Noble in 1994 all tried to find interesting ways of presenting the play without imitating Brook. They were not the only RSC directors to essay the *Dream*, but in some ways they were the most significant. In part, they all succeeded in what they set out to do. Barton chose to go in a direction opposite to Brook's and produced a more traditional *Dream*. By contrast, Daniels tried to find a mean between the extremes of tradition and revolution. He began conventionally but then resorted to doubling the major roles and using large, wooden puppets (adapted from Japanese techniques) for the fairies. Alexander doubled Hippolyta with Titania—it was Hippolyta's dream, in his interpretation— but not Theseus and Oberon. William Dudley designed the set in what was referred to as the "post-Rackham, post-Dulac period."[56]

Adrian Noble was perhaps the most imaginative of the four, while at the same time paying tribute to Brook's achievement three decades earlier. His stage was, like Brook's, almost entirely bare, but it featured a far more colorful red box instead of Jacobs's stark white one. In place of trees, dozens of lightbulbs dropped from above, giving the appropriate illusion in the central scenes (compare Brook's wires). Titania's bower was a large, soft, pink, inverted umbrella which descended from above— another reminiscence of Brook's *Dream*, along with the swing stage right on which Hippolyta sat at the beginning of 1.1. Otherwise, except for two smaller, green umbrellas (also inverted), on which Puck and the First Fairy rose from below, no further props were used. He followed Brook in doubling the major roles, but he went farther and doubled the mechanicals and the four fairies. His overarching concept for the *Dream* was dream, a descent into the unconscious.[57]

OTHER POST-BROOK DREAMS

Perhaps the most astonishing *Dream* after Brook's—both a striking re-action against it as well as a tribute to it—was Robert Lepage's produc-tion given at London's Royal National Theatre in 1992. Like Brook, Lepage set out to overturn all preconceptions concerning the play and its performance. His set, designed by Michael Levine, was a large, shal-low, circular pool of water, surrounded by a bank of mud, beyond which was a running track of somewhat firmer material. Here the lovers could race around during the forest scenes, when they were not splashing about in the water and mud (the production was thus nicknamed "A Mudsum-mer Night's Dream"). For Levine, the mud was "a purely sensual idea" as well as a metaphor: "the characters, getting dirtier by the minute, become embroiled in the complications of the plot and, literally, to wal-low in experience"[58] Director, designer, and cast, moreover, saw in the text of *A Midsummer Night's Dream* a good many references to floods and tempests, all of which confirmed their intuitions that water was cen-tral to the play, as mud was to the primordial experiences the play con-veyed (see Halio 1994, 118–19).

The performance began with a strange creature dressed in scarlet, one breast exposed, crawling crabwise across the stage to the center of the pool. This was Puck, played by a Canadian acrobat and contortionist, Angela Laurier, walking on her hands with her feet over her shoulders. When she got directly under the single lightbulb that hung suspended by a cord, she reached up and turned it off. Blackout. Puck then scurried off, and when the lights came back on, the action of the play proper began. Theseus and Hippolyta entered perched on a brass bedstead,[59] pushed onto the pool by the four young lovers and followed on foot by Egeus and Philostrate, who later poled the bed around the pool. As The-seus and Hippolyta situated themselves at the bedhead, the lovers got aboard and lay down at the other end; their posture clearly suggested that they were asleep. What ensued, therefore, could be understood as their collective dream.[60] Everyone wore white, light clothing—Theseus and Hippolyta in flowing robes, the young lovers in what looked like nighties and pajamas. The fairies, who entered later, wore blue paint on their faces and dressed in black, both to distinguish them from the mor-tals and to suggest their otherworldly state. Titania and Oberon appeared as Eastern potentates, though not encumbered with heavy garments. A gamelan orchestra provided what music there was.

The production was highly physical, sometimes at the expense of the text, although Lepage cut very little. Some critics complained that Shakespeare's language got lost among all the shenanigans, as when the lovers splashed about in the pool.[61] Bottom did not wear an ass's head, quite; instead, Puck mounted on his back with legs upraised over his head to suggest donkey ears. Unfortunately, Laurier's French accent obscured some of her words, although her physical versatility partly compensated for that. In truth, with so much physical behavior to attend to, both audiences and performers had difficulty in concentrating on what was said as well as what was done, or rather how what was done reflected or enacted what was said. This was a primary difference between Lepage's *Dream* and Brook's (Halio 1994, 122).

England was by no means the sole source of innovative and interesting productions of *A Midsummer Night's Dream*. By the end of the twentieth century, countless productions all over the world had proved how fascinating and durable Shakespeare's play is, not only on stage but also on the large and small screens. Between 1971 and 1978 alone, for instance, more than eighteen productions were mounted in what was then called the German Democratic Republic, two of them almost simultaneously in East Berlin in 1980. While some revealed Brook's influence, others veered off in quite different directions. Christopher Schroth's production in Halle (1971), for instance, emphasized "the individual struggle for freedom as reflected in all its complexity." If Athens was a "rigid, closed, intact society that curtails human potentiality," the wood was its "mythologically alienated, distorted reflection," where courtly rigidity could give way to "the freedom of uninhibited passion."[62] Strips of white cloth, which hung in orderly, vertical rows to suggest classical Greek columns in Athens, gave way to a "jungle of treetrunks through which Athenians stagger as in a labyrinth."[63] By contrast, modernism and dynamics were the keynotes of Werner Freese's production in Magdeburg, also in 1971. Harmony overcoming disharmony was its major theme, with the "erotic urge" as a primary motivation for the action. Far from a jungle, the forest was represented by large metal structures resembling pieces of jewelry (Hamburger 1988, 52–54).

Most impressive, perhaps, was Alexander Lang's *Dream* presented at the Deutsches Theater in East Berlin in 1980. The entire production was staged like a dream within a dream, as the performers rose up from a deep sleep singing "Sommerkanon" (a version of "Sumer is icumen in") at the beginning and "Winteraustreiben" (a song about driving winter out) at the end. The latter replaced the Bergomask and blessing of the house in Shakespeare's script, and afterward everyone went back to sleep. The stage was simply a box with red paper walls for both court and forest, suggesting that the action took place within the unconscious. As Lang explained, "The forest is within the people." It required no special scenic design, since the structure of human relationships was of paramount importance.

Male chauvinism in Lang's production knew no bounds, and the eroticism was "more alienating than extenuating."[64] According to Williams, Lang's production offered "a polemical indictment of the state and the disparities between social reality and government versions of it" (1997, 236). In the forest, for example, manipulations of the state seemed to underlie the uses of the love potion.

Politics also influenced later German productions of *A Midsummer Night's Dream*, for example, in Karin Beier's staging for the Dusseldorf Schauspielhaus in 1995–96. She used fourteen actors speaking nine different languages to present a kind of postmodern Babel to suggest the difficult efforts being made in Europe to establish a new union. "When the characters were not caught up in language confusions and cultural differences, they seemed to be subjects in the thrall of a cruel sexuality, as has been the case in a number of postmodern productions" (Williams 1997, 254). Her concept grew out of her idea, according to Williams, of a European Shakespeare, the result of a 1995 directors' workshop sponsored by the Union of European Theatres. This experiment was not very successful and most likely had unintended as well as intentional comic effects, as in 1.1 when English-speaking Hermia (Penny Needler) swore by "Cupid's strongest bow" incomprehensibly to Hebrew-speaking Lysander. She ultimately had to resort to flapping her arms like wings to convey what she meant (255).

Far more successful and less political was Daniel Yang's lavish Chinese production of *A Midsummer Night's Dream* in Hong Kong in 1997, later revived and somewhat altered for Taipei in 2000. These were not the first Chinese productions of the play; Xong Yuan Wei, for instance, had directed the *Dream* in Beijing in 1988. His production was acted as spoken drama mixed with stage techniques of traditional Chinese theater. According to one observer, the result was "a lyrical and romantic atmosphere with an Asian flavor."[65] Although Yang's knowledge of traditional Chinese theater is considerable as is his fluency in the language, he had a long experience in the West as a director of Shakespeare's plays and as the artistic director of the Colorado Shakespeare Festival in

Oberon, Titania, and Puck in Daniel Yang's Chinese production (2000). Courtesy of Daniel Yang.

the United States. He knew at first hand many excellent English and American productions of Shakespeare. His production, therefore, used many Western techniques of staging and presentation, while based on a Chinese translation of the text that he himself had made.

Yang's production was set in a mythical locale with a hint of contemporary Hong Kong. Athens became merely "the Capital." Theseus, who also doubled as Oberon, first appeared in a cape of royal purple spangled at the shoulders and wore a round, triple-layered crown, like an abbreviated mitre. Hippolyta, wearing a red gown, seemed happy enough—not at all like the discontented Hippolytas of some Western productions, although she later doubled as Titania. The courtier's military uniforms and formal dresses suggested a nineteenth-century milieu; the lovers wore simpler costumes. Workmen looked very much like contemporary laborers, as in Wei's production. The fairies in Titania's train were four-season flowers; those following Oberon were beetles and other insects. Titania's costume resembled a white lily; Oberon's, a king beetle, with Puck as a junior version of that image. In the original staging of this production, the basic setting consisted of a multileveled, forty-five-foot revolve with a yin-yang motif, if seen from the top; but for the revival

Titania in her bower, with Puck and fairies, in Daniel Yang's Chinese production. Courtesy of Daniel Yang.

held in 2000, the setting was simplified. A single-level, forty-five-foot raked disk was substituted for the main playing area, supplemented by curved wall portals on both sides as surfaces for projection. The raked disk was also the surface for complicated lighting patterns and projections.

To create the world of the forest and to emphasize the magic of the fairy world, Yang asked his designer to lower thirty-six neon tubes, in different combinations and permutations, to supplement the raked disk on the floor as additional scenic units. These neon tubes changed into rainbow colors as moods and locales changed. The green was reserved for the forest scenes, blue for Oberon and Puck, and a mixed color for Titania—for example, pink for the moment when she fell in love with Bottom. Yellow was used, appropriately, for the rising sun in 4.1. According to Yang, he got the idea for these scenic effects from Wagner's Bayreuth Festival, where he saw the Ring Cycle performed. The idea of hanging lights, or tubes, is reminiscent of Xong's hanging ropes and Noble's lightbulbs, used to suggest the forest environment. Overall, then, Yang's Chinese production of the *Dream* combined beautifully and spectacularly modern Western design techniques with Mandarin speaking and Chinese facial expressions and movement.

THE GLOBE ONCE MORE

In the summer of 2002, *A Midsummer Night's Dream* returned to the bankside, where it had been performed four centuries earlier. At the reconstructed Globe Theatre, the Red Company directed by Mike Alfreds performed their version of Shakespeare's comedy before audiences seated in the galleries or standing in the yard. Although many productions at the new Globe since its opening several years earlier tried to replicate the conditions and production techniques of the Elizabethan era, using all male casts, for example (though men, not boys, in women's roles), this production made several concessions to modern staging. Women played the roles of Hermia and Helena, and Geraldine Alexander doubled as Hippolyta and Titania. Since some performances were held at night, artificial lighting had to be used—to illuminate the entire theater, not only the stage—replicating as far as possible the effect of open-air daylight performances. In addition, two intervals broke the playing time; the performance lasted about three hours all told.

The stage was essentially bare, of course. Costumes were simple. The lovers wore pajamas which became more and more disheveled during their forest experience. Quince & Co., in workmen's clothes, also doubled as the fairies, as probably they did in some of the original stagings of the play in the public theaters. As fairies they wore little lights over their torsos, which twinkled appropriately to suggest their otherworldliness. Bottom, transformed, did not wear an ass's head exactly; his "ears" were ladies fur-trimmed slippers strapped on end over his ears, and on his nose, he wore a white cup. The costuming for "Pyramus and Thisbe" was also kept simple. Lion wore a large yellow ruff; Wall was bare chested and carried a sheet. Pyramus came on with a beard made of shaving cream lather, which evoked laughter whenever it rubbed off on another actor through deliberate or inadvertent contact.

Musicians were placed not above in the Lord's Room, but on the main stage in the discovery space, so that they were in view constantly. The text was only lightly cut. Some words were altered—needlessly, it seemed. For example, when Bottom says he will "aggravate" his voice to play the lion (1.2.66), we hear, rather, that he will "constipate" his voice. Later he is not "translated" but "transcommunicated." On the other hand, the lullaby in 2.2 was beautifully sung, and when Oberon and Titania were reconciled, they performed a lovely, tango-like dance. No Bergomask followed the play-within-the-play, but Oberon sang his blessing at the end as the fairies danced and joined in as chorus.

Thus *A Midsummer Night's Dream* once more graced the south bank of the Thames, bringing full circle, as it were, the performance history of this magnificent Shakespearean comedy.

NOTES

1. E. K. Chambers, *The Elizabethan Stage*. Oxford: Clarendon Press, 1924, 3: 279. See also Gary Jay Williams, *Our Moonlight Revels: "A Midsummer Night's Dream in the Theatre*. Iowa City: University of Iowa Press, 1997, 36; and Jay L. Halio, *Shakespeare in Performance: A Midsummer Night's Dream*. Manchester, England: Manchester University Press, 1994, 13.

2. Cited by Williams, *Moonlight Revels*, 36.

3. See G. E. Bentley, *Jacobean and Caroline Drama*. Oxford: Oxford University Press, 1941–68, 1: 27; also Williams, *Moonlight Revels*, 36; and Halio, *Shakespeare in Performance*, 13.

4. E. K. Chambers, *William Shakespeare*. Oxford: Clarendon Press, 1930, 2: 348–52; cited by Williams, *Moonlight Revels*, 36.

5. On doubling, see William Ringler, "The Number of Actors in Shakespeare's Early Plays," in *The Seventeenth-Century Stage*, ed. G. E. Bentley 110–34, esp. 130–34. Chicago: University of Chicago Press, 1968. Ringler believes that four of the mechanicals—Flute, Starveling, Snout, and Snug—could have doubled as the fairies Peaseblossom, Cobweb, Moth, and Mustardseed; in fact, such doubling has been done in some modern productions, as in Adrian Noble's RSC production in 1994 (see 118). Ringler does not think the actors playing Theseus and Hippolyta doubled as Oberon and Titania, as in a later adaptation of the play in 1673; as Brook cast them in his 1970 production, and as many later productions followed suit. See also T. J. King, *Casting Shakespeare's Plays*. Cambridge, England: Cambridge University Press, 1992, 6; and Williams, *Moonlight Revels*, 32–34.

6. See Ronald Watkins and Jeremy Lemmon, *In Shakespeare's Playhouse: "A Midsummer Night's Dream."* Totowa, N.J.: Humanities Press, 1974, 17.

7. "Act" at that time could refer to the intermission between acts. See Williams, *Moonlight Revels*, 25.

8. Ibid., 23.

9. Watkins and Lemmon, *Shakespeare's Playhouse*, 52.

10. See Minor White Latham, *The Elizabethan Fairies*. New York: Columbia University Press, 1930, 219–23, 239–45.

11. "The mingling of fairyland and classical figures was common in fairy traditions of the age, and we may suspect that the dressing of Titania and her train echoes that of the classical sylphs" (Williams, *Moonlight Revels*, 28). Williams cites further evidence to suggest that Titania and her train may have been dressed in flowing green or white robes, perhaps winged and masked, and

Oberon's costume could have been a fantastic mixture of knightly armor and Greco-Roman elements, also perhaps winged (31). See the illustrations of Inigo Jones's costumes for Jonson's *Masque of Oberon* on pp. 29–30 of Williams, *Moonlight Revels*.

12. Ibid., 27–28. Williams believes the costumes were a blend of Greco-Roman and knightly elements.

13. See Watkins and Lemmon, *Shakespeare's Playhouse*, 26–17.

14. Cited by Halio, *Shakespeare in Performance*, 13–14.

15. Quoted in George C. Odell, *Shakespeare from Betterton to Irving*. New York: Scribner's, 1920, 1: 40–41.

16. A facsimile of this edition was published by the Cornmarket Press in 1969. Tonson's edition does not give Purcell's music, now available in a form adapted for modern voices among Edwin F. Kalmus's vocal scores (No. 6868, New York, n.d.), which includes the additions of 1693.

17. See Halio, *Shakespeare in Performance*, 16, for an example of this refining tendency; compare Williams, *Moonlight Revels*, 45. On pp. 46–60, Williams gives a detailed analysis of the opera.

18. Montague Summers, *The Restoration Theatre*. New York: Macmillan, 1934, 235.

19. Before that, bits and pieces of *A Midsummer Night's Dream* appeared in such afterpieces as Richard Leveridge's *Comick Masque of Pyramus and Thisbe*, a spoof of Italian opera then popular in London. See Williams, *Moonlight Revels*, 62.

20. George Winchester Stone, "*A Midsummer Night's Dream* in the Hands of Garrick and Colman," *PMLA* 54 (1939), 474.

21. See Charles B. Hogan, *Shakespeare in the Theatre, 1701–1800*. Oxford: Oxford University Press, 1957, 2: 471–72.

22. Ibid., 2: 473.

23. Cited by Gamani Salgado, *Eyewitnesses of Shakespeare*. New York: Barnes and Noble, 1975, 117. See also Odell, *Shakespeare*, 2: 111–12.

24. See Halio, *Shakespeare in Performance*, 21–22, who cites the promptbook in the Folger Shakespeare Library (MND 18). For a detailed description of this adaptation, see Williams, *Moonlight Revels*, 77–80, 86–91. Williams explains the martial conclusion in terms of British colonial discourse and notes that 1816 was the year following Napoléon Bonaparte's defeat at Waterloo. See pp. 80–86.

25. See Odell, *Shakespeare*, 2: 147; and Williams, *Moonlight Revels*, 91–92.

26. See Trevor Griffiths, "A Neglected Pioneer Production: Madame Vestris' *A Midsummer Night's Dream*," *Shakespeare Quarterly* 30 (1979), 386–96; and Williams, *Moonlight Revels*, 93–103.

27. See Williams, *Moonlight Revels*, 98, for details.

28. See Halio, *Shakespeare in Performance*, 24–25; and Williams, *Moonlight Revels*, 99.

29. Griffiths, "Neglected Pioneer Production," 390; see also Halio, *Shakespeare in Performance*, 24–25. In Lepage's production at the National Theatre, London, in 1992, for example, Angela Laurier played Puck.

30. The material in this paragraph derives from Williams, *Moonlight Revels*, 103–9.

31. Henry Morley, *Journal of a London Playgoer, from 1851 to 1866*. London, 1891, 57.

32. See Richard Foulkes, "Samuel Phelps's *A Midsummer Night's Dream*: Sadler's Wells—October 8th, 1853," *Theatre Notebook* 23 (1968–69), 55–60.

33. Williams (*Moonlight Revels*, 295, n. 10) suspects that Phelps used Mendelssohn's music from the first, although no composer credit is given on the 1853 playbills he has seen.

34. See Charles Shattuck, *Shakespeare on the American Stage: From the Hallams to Edwin Booth*. Washington, D.C.: Folger Books, 1976, 89.

35. See Williams (*Moonlight Revels*, 122–25), who gives further details of Keene's productions and those of others, especially their scenic effects, where spectacle was the "star" (123).

36. See Halio, *Shakespeare in Performance*, 28–29; and Williams, *Moonlight Revels*, 122–24.

37. George C. Odell, *Annals of the New York Stage*. New York: Columbia University Press, 1927–49, 1: 280–81.

38. George Bernard Shaw, *Dramatic Opinions and Essays*. London: Constable, 1906, 1: 173–76.

39. Cited by Odell, *Shakespeare*, 2: 454.

40. See Robert Speaight, *Shakespeare on the Stage*. Boston: Little, Brown, 1973, 125.

41. J. C. Trewin, *Shakespeare on the English Stage, 1900–1964*. London: Barrie and Rockliff, 1964, 4–5.

42. As late as 1954, when London's Old Vic and Sadler's Wells Ballet teamed up under Michael Benthall's direction, a whole forest of trees appeared on stage for the central acts, and a sixty-piece orchestra played Mendelssohn's music. Robert Helpmann played—and danced—Oberon; Moira Shearer, Titania. The production opened at the Edinburgh Opera House and a month later at New York City's old Metropolitan Opera House, from where it toured major U.S. and Canadian cities (Halio, *Shakespeare in Performance*, 43).

43. See John L. Styan, *The Shakespeare Revolution*. Cambridge, England: Cambridge University Press, 1977, 84.

44. See Halio, *Shakespeare in Performance*, 33; and Styan, *Shakespeare Revolution*, 84–85.

45. Halio, *Shakespeare in Performance*, 33–34, citing Styan, *Shakespeare Revolution*, 99; and Trewin, *English Stage*, 57.

46. John L. Styan, *Max Reinhardt*. Cambridge, England: Cambridge University Press, 1982, 56–60; see also Halio, *Shakespeare in Performance*, 38.

47. For an account of a revival, see Anna Kisselgoff, "On Wings of Mendelssohn and Shakespeare," *New York Times*, February 13, 1993, 11.

48. For a fuller account of this production, see Halio, *Shakespeare in Performance*, 44–45; and Arthur Gelb, "Shakespeare Rides the Range in Texan 'Dream,' " *New York Times*, April 1, 1959, 44.

49. See Glen Loney, *Peter Brook's Production of William Shakespeare's "A Midsummer Night's Dream" for the Royal Shakespeare Company: The Complete and Authorized Acting Edition*. Stratford-upon-Avon, England: Royal Shakespeare Company, 1974, 24.

50. Except when performing "Pyramus and Thisbe," the mechanicals wore more realistic costumes, clothes of contemporary workmen, to contrast with the others, as the play demands (Halio, *Shakespeare in Performance*, 57).

51. See Peter Brook, *The Shifting Point*. New York, 1987, 96–97, for his conception of the fairies as related to the Chinese circus.

52. In Ralph Berry, *On Directing Shakespeare*. 2d ed. London: Hamish Hamilton, 1989, 151.

53. David Selbourne, *The Making of "A Midsummer Night's Dream."* London: Methuen, 1982, 5.

54. "Dream 2001 AD," *Statesman*, September 4, 1970.

55. "Free Shakespeare," *Shakespeare Survey* 24 (1971), 133.

56. See John Higgins, "Dreaming for Everyone," an interview with William Dudley and Bill Alexander, [London] *Times*, June 30, 1986, 19. For more on this production and others, see Halio, *Shakespeare in Performance*, 72–82; and Williams, *Moonlight Revels*, 242–47, 251–52.

57. For more on this production, see the second edition of Halio's *Shakespeare in Performance: A Midsummer Night's Dream*. Manchester, England: Manchester University Press, 2003, ch. 8.

58. See Heather Neill, "Dream and Nightmare Meet," [London] *Times*, July 2, 1992.

59. This bed proved to be very versatile. Upended, for example, it served as the entrance to the mechanicals' house in 4.2.

60. George L. Geckle, review of production, *Shakespeare Bulletin* 11 (1993), 27.

61. See, for instance, Geckle (ibid., 28); and Malcolm Rutherford's review in *Financial Times*, July 11, 1992.

62. Maik Hamburger, "New Concepts in Staging 'A Midsummer Night's Dream,' " *Shakespeare Survey* 40 (1988), 52.

63. Ibid., 52–53; compare Williams, *Moonlight Revels*, 236, who notes how the lovers were terribly confused by their passions, whereas "a fully developed, complex Bottom" had "a great capacity for love."

64. Martin Linzer, "*A Midsummer Night's Dream* in East Germany," trans. Brigitte Kueppers, *Drama Review* 25 (1981), 46.

65. Xiao Yang Zhang, *Shakespeare in China*. Newark: University of Delaware Press, 1996, 169.

7

THE PLAY ON FILM

During the silent film era, directors and producers turned to Shakespeare's plays for scripts. Between 1908 and 1911 alone, they made fifty Shakespeare films, including a one-reeler in 1909 by the Vitagraph Company of the perennially popular *A Midsummer Night's Dream*. In 1935 Max Reinhardt teamed up with William Dieterle to make the first full-length sound film of the play. It featured Victor Jory as Oberon, Mickey Rooney as Puck, Anita Louise as Titania, and James Cagney as Bottom. Other well-known film actors, such as Dick Powell (Lysander), Olivia de Haviland (Hermia), and Joe E. Brown (Flute), also appeared in what was, in effect, an all-star cast. Though most of the stars had little or no experience playing Shakespeare or speaking his lines, they had considerable box office appeal and were highly photogenic.

For this film, as for most Shakespearean films then and now, the text was severely cut, but some of the play's darker aspects were preserved.[1] Mendelssohn's music was used extensively. The film was shot in black and white. Some new scenes were interpolated; for example, at the beginning, a poster announces Theseus's forthcoming wedding and a prize is offered for the best play performed in celebration of the event. A great procession led by Theseus winds its way through Athens, as the camera switches between long shots and close-ups of the principal characters, including Hermia and Lysander waving to each other across crowds of cheering people, while Demetrius receives scowls from Hermia and wistful looks from Helena. Quince and his fellows are also there, planning how to present their play. Hippolyta, defeated and downcast, appears in Theseus's train with a large snake coiled about her.

Otis Harlan as Starveling, Hugh Hubert as Snout, Frank McHugh as Quince, Joe E. Brown (in background) as Flute, James Cagney as Bottom, Arthur Treacher as Ninny's Tomb, and Dewey Robinson as Snug in the Reinhardt-Dieterle film (1936). Courtesy of Photofest.

After Theseus and Hippolyta ride off in a chariot to Mendelssohn's "Wedding March," Hermia and Lysander embrace and Helena woos Demetrius. Egeus immediately breaks in and disrupts his daughter's happiness, commanding her (in dialogue transposed from 1.1) to marry Demetrius, while Helena weeps. The scene thus forms a kind of prologue to the play, whose action proper begins in the following scene, set in Theseus's ornate palace. Hippolyta, dressed in a rich, black gown, paces silently, until Theseus approaches and speaks of their impending nuptials. Reinhardt does not make much of this relationship, though it is quite evident that Hippolyta's position is that of a captured Amazon queen.

When Egeus enters with the lovers, he presents his case to the duke, who with great dignity supports Egeus's claims. Hermia runs off, distraught; Hippolyta's reaction is not shown. Lysander follows his lover and speaks his lines on "The course of true love," while a hidden orchestra plays "Love in Bloom"—one of the most banal moments in the film. Passionate Hermia agrees to elope with Lysander, and the scene shifts to Peter Quince's carpentry shop for the casting of "Pyramus and Thisbe."

James Cagney as Bottom is extremely volatile. He conveys his interpretation of Bottom's asinine egocentricity by three times repeating, with increasing wonderment, "I play Pyramus"; but laughter erupts immediately afterward when he asks, "What is Pyramus?" Joe E. Brown's Flute, who eats sunflower seeds and spits out the husks, is unimpressed throughout. Quince has trouble reading the script, which later explains his difficulty with the Prologue at court. A roaring match between Bottom and Snug, who plays Lion, revives an old piece of stage business and is only faintly amusing.

In 2.1 Shakespeare's poetry is made visual, as the camera focuses on the sky, animals, birds, streams, and trees, while Mendelssohn's music plays. Puck awakens and rises from a heap of leaves, then summons his pony. Adults play the fairies, who emerge from the mists and dance upward on a spiral of fog, or a moonbeam—a special cinematic effect. The Indian boy appears in a turban and silks, "like a miniature Rajah . . . looking as though he wandered into Shakespeare's woods . . . from the set of a Kipling film."[2] He runs after a group of fairies, who fly off after being fightened by a water troll. He tries to follow by flapping his arms helplessly—another banal moment. The fairies later find him swinging on a branch and place him on a unicorn. All this time, an orchestra of gnomes or goblens play Mendelssohn's "Scherzo."

This gives the reader some idea of Hollywood's early rendering of Shakespeare's play. Some of the acting and the interpretation of roles are actually quite good. Jory's Oberon is appropriately sinister, and Anita Louise's Titania, lovely to behold, treats the King of Fairies with a light-hearted disdain. Puck is suitably puckish. At Oberon's command, Puck wanders through the forest bareback on his pony looking for the lovers, and he occasionally addresses the audience directly, as if to invite them to enjoy his mischief, too. The young lovers both sadly and comically embody his comment, "What fools these mortals be" (3.12.115).

The ass's head Puck places on Bottom unfortunately looks much too artificial, like something taken from a carousel or merry-go-round, though it otherwise serves sufficiently to frighten Quince and the others. Titania's lovemaking, however, becomes much too ludicrous. Again, Reinhardt here interpolates some foolish stage business, making the Indian boy turn away sorrowfully, as if rejected by witnessing Titania's new love. A mock wedding takes place to the parodied strains of Mendelssohn's "Wedding March," anticipating by thirty-five years Brook's similar staging. During this episode, Oberon sees the opportunity to seize the boy, now abandoned and crying, and carry him off on his horse—an action that differs from Shakespeare's account in the text.

Meanwhile, Titania sings to Bottom, who neighs in rhythm with her and falls asleep in her arms. Oberon later appears with the Indian boy on his horse; he takes pity on Titania and soon removes her spell. His cape billows behind him, under which troops of elves and batmen follow. Elsewhere, the sleeping lovers stir briefly and smile, while fairies, herded like slaves by Oberon's henchmen, dance and disappear under Oberon's cloak. While the gnome orchestra plays Mendelssohn's "Nocturne," First Fairy and a batman perform a pas de deux, or a duel between Moonlight and Night—a surrealistic ballet with strong sexual overtones—yet another Reinhardt interpolation.[3]

The young lovers awaken, but not by the sound of Theseus's hounds. They laugh hilariously as they seem to recall their "dream" and run off to join the procession moving toward Athens with Theseus and Hippolyta on a float. Egeus is furious when he sees the couples, but Theseus silences him and invites the young people to join in the wedding ceremonies. The speeches about his hounds and the tricks of the imagination have both been cut. Once inside the palace, a great banquet is served, and Quince & Co. arrive with their costumes and props. Puck enters "invisibly" and so confuses Philostrate that he mistakenly hands Theseus "Pyramus and Thisbe" as the play to be performed.

The play-within-the-play is the weakest part of the film, for it drags on too long and is filled with too much slapstick. After it ends, the audience sneaks away rather than watch the Bergomask, to the dismay of the mechanicals. Puck then blows out a candle, and in the darkness Oberon and Titania fly in with the fairies to bless the house. Afterward, Puck extinguishes all the lights, and through a circular opening in a scrim he delivers the epilogue.

For all its faults, the Reinhardt-Dieterle film accomplished a good deal. It shows how, used imaginatively, film can translate Shakespeare's verse to visual beauty. It has the added advantage of presenting intimate close-ups in various scenes with the kind of directness that is far more difficult to attain on stage in live performances. These advantages compensate, at least in part, for the obvious disadvantage of having to cater to a mass audience and use actors whose skill enacting Shakespeare is minimal, or worse. That disadvantage, however, is not a necessary one, as Peter Hall's film proved.

Everything in Hall's film (1968) is different from Reinhardt's. To begin with, Hall cast the leads with well-trained Shakespearean actors: Derek Godfrey as Theseus, Barbara Jefford as Hippolyta, Ian Richardson as Oberon, Judi Dench as Titania, Diana Rigg as Helena, Helen Mirren as Helena, Ian Holm as Puck, and Sebastian Shaw as Quince. Many of them had appeared in Hall's 1962 stage production, which he carefully and adroitly adapted for the film medium. He used color photography, and instead of using Mendelssohn's music, he added a new score composed by Guy Wolfenden. Hall's aim "was to project an earthy, erotic comedy with a strong flavor of Warwickshire in its setting—Athens in rural England."[4] Unlike Reinhardt, he kept Shakespeare's text almost entirely intact. Moreover, he resisted overly spectacular effects and excessively burlesquing by the mechanicals. With its emphasis on language and action, it is one of the best Shakespearean films ever made.

Like Reinhardt, Hall introduced a "director's overture" (Jorgens 1977, 52) to set the atmosphere and tone. The English landscape appears in rain and fog to the sound of distant horns, as the screen credits roll. As the day clears, a dignified, solitary figure—Philostrate—strolls purposefully across the lawn to a stately country house (Compton Verney, Warwickshire). In this fashion, Hall contrasts the symbol of human civility and order with the images of disordered nature shown previously (52–53).

The camera cuts to Theseus and Hippolyta, who, alone, are leaning on a balustrade of their country home overlooking a formal garden. This Hippolyta accepts her conquest by Theseus and seems to look forward with him to their impending nuptials. The camera then cuts abruptly indoors, where Egeus appears with the young lovers and denounces his daughter. A wise and compassionate ruler, Theseus listens and advises Hermia to obey her father's wishes or suffer the consequences. He then leads all but Hermia and Lysander away, leaving the lovers alone to consult with each other.

Hall breaks this part of the dialogue in 1.1 by shifting its later lines to the lovers seated in a boat on the water. When Helena appears on the shore, they join her and reveal their plan to elope. Helena's soliloquy is delivered directly to the camera, which then switches to the next scene set in a farmyard with the mechanicals planning to perform a play for the duke. Workmen who seem to have come right out of the Warwickshire countryside, they are on their lunch break. Peter Quince is rather prim and fussy but uses all of his rustic charm when dealing with Bottom (Paul Rogers). The scene then changes to the dream world of the forest.

It is night. An owl hoots, as a fairy runs along tossing glitter (stardust, perhaps?) here and there. Hall's fairies are little boys and girls with smudged faces and ragamuffin clothes, like characters out of *Peter Pan*—all except, of course, Oberon, Titania, and Puck. Through a rapid succession of camera shots focusing on animals, fairies dashing through the forest, Titania and Oberon running, then stopping and facing each other, Hall establishes the magical world of nature. Hardly a benign pastoral landscape, it contrasts directly with Theseus's restrained, orderly world and soon evolves into "a mirror for the confusion and pull of sexual and gender loyalties experienced by the lovers" who enter it.[5] Oberon and Titania are almost naked: she, very curvaceous, sensual, and sexy; he, slim and sinister, with a pointed goatee, satyr-like except for his otherwise smooth-skinned, greenish body. Their nudity and the weird camera effects they inspire link them to the wood demons of Elizabethan folklore.

Hall distinguishes the fairies from the mortals primarily by body makeup, usually a greenish hue with contrasting red lips. Color sequences alternate rapidly from red to blue or orange as backgrounds for Oberon's and Titania's speeches. The only unfortunate aspect of the entire film is Puck's panting like a dog eager to carry out Oberon's orders. In every other respect, Hall succeeds in presenting this nighttime world as the dream world Shakespeare intended. When Helena and Demetrius enter it, they pass right beside "invisible" Oberon and crawl through the underbrush, already becoming sweaty and scratched. Demetrius tries to run off, but Helena chases him and holds him in a half nelson while she pleads her love (2.1.229 ff.). Oberon pities her and promises that her love will be requited.

By not showing Titania's bower as Oberon speaks the lines describing it, Hall evidently preferred to let Shakespeare's imagery do its own work. In any case, the bower appears in the next scene, when Titania settles down to rest. Her fairies sing their lullaby, some playing on wooden pipes, grotesque horns, and other rustic instruments. After they leave her asleep and her cobwebby sentinel is hit on the head and drops to the ground, Oberon and Puck appear to apply love-in-idleness on her eyes. An owl hoots again, and nightbirds sing. Perhaps with an eventual television broadcast in mind, Hall chose to emphasize the comedy and sensuality of sex, not its brutality, at least here.

Hall shows how awful the lovers' plight is, first and last, after they enter the forest. For example, when Hermia awakens crying and frightened by her dream (2.2.151–62), her distress is real. Later on, after Demetrius finds her, they are both besplattered and upset, moving through a thicket and wading in a stream. At one point, exasperated by his wooing, Hermia pushes him into the water. To this extent, Hall shows a willingness to portray love's violence, somewhat downplaying the comedy here as the lovers emerge more and more begrimed with mud and their clothes torn. When Helena speaks of how she and Hermia were once "Two lovely berries moulded on one stem" (3.2.211), the camera focuses on the women sitting close together, very much "Like to a double cherry, seeming parted" (209). But the tender moment passes, giving way to anger, ambiguity dissolving into conflict. The young women, like the men, have at each other; Helena comically climbs a tree, and Hermia displays deep anguish when Lysander scorns her.

In contrast, the mechanicals' experience in the forest is characterized by broad comedy. Puck turns up, ready for mischief. Bottom's ass's head is more realistic than Cagney's in Reinhardt's film; its hairy face blends in with the hair on Rogers's own scalp. After his friends, badly frightened, run off in comic confusion, Bottom sings to himself, loudly and off-key, which awakens Titania, who begins to woo him. The weaver vainly tries to escape, but Titania blocks him with her body, and her fairies arrive to lead him to her bower. There, Titania lowers him to the ground and embraces him amorously, preparatory to sexual intercourse.

Hall does not picture the act, which is hardly necessary. Eventually, Oberon takes pity on his queen as she continues to fondle Bottom and his grotesque head. When he releases her from the charm, she kisses him and turns in tears and loathing to observe Bottom still sleeping in her bower. Music sounds; she and Oberon kiss and dance a courtly measure. When Puck announces that he hears the lark, they run off together deeper into the forest. Meanwhile, having seen the young lovers in all their difficulties, Oberon orders his minion to set things right. As in Reinhardt's film, Puck blows fog over the scene, and by a flick of his hand sends all the lovers to sleep, dropping a bit of hay on them and kissing the women before each one falls out of the frame—a neat cinematic effect. As they lie asleep, Helena with her thumb in her mouth, Puck removes the spell from Lysander and reassures the camera audience that "all shall be well" (3.2.461–63).

Hall retains the hunting scene but underplays it. Theseus and Hippolyta walk, not ride, to the hounds. Awakened by Theseus's horns, Hermia and Lysander kiss—like Oberon and Titania in "new amity" (4.1.84)— and Helena and Demetrius also rise. They all then kneel before Theseus and explain as well as they can what has happened to them. Theseus overbears an angry Egeus and declares a triple wedding shall be held. Bottom awakes, his ass's head gone, and he addresses the camera, trying to explain his "rare vision" with a nice balance of wonder and rustic wit. Here as elsewhere the camera in close-up is highly effective. Hall then for the first and only time transposes a scene, shifting now to Athens and Theseus's speech on the imagination so that it immediately follows Bottom's soliloquy. The camera next cuts to Quince's shed, where the mechanicals bemoan their friend's absence. Suddenly dogs bark, and Bottom appears, yelling his greeting and announcing his good news that their play is preferred.

Hall's restraint and measured pace are especially evident in the final scene. As the court gathers for the entertainment, a tiny stage is set up in Theseus's hall. The courtiers, seated, await the performance, while servants sit on the stairs to watch. Over Philostrate's snobbish objections, the duke chooses "Pyramus and Thisbe" to be played. Here as elsewhere, Hall shaves a few speeches, cutting about eighty lines all told from act 5, more than in any previous scene. The courtiers' quips remain, delivered more or less genially, until almost the end of the performance, when even Theseus becomes exasperated, though the farcical enactment proceeds with rather less slapstick and a kind of earnestness that becomes almost endearing. For instance, Thisbe drops his high falsetto when he sees Pyramus dead, and his suicide is most affecting. During the Bergomask, only Bottom and Flute dance, while the others provide the music with their rustic instruments.

After chimes announce midnight, better music sounds. Theseus thanks the performers and summons everyone to bed. Puck in close-up delivers his soliloquy (5.1.349–68), and then fairies enter the house, popping up from behind chairs. Oberon and Titania kiss, and everyone lights tapers. To the sound of horns, as at the beginning of the film, and singing, Oberon and Titania mount the stairs, whereupon Oberon blesses the house and throws glitter; then everyone exits. An owl hoots once more as the camera moves outside and focuses on the darkened house. Suddenly, Puck appears and delivers his epilogue, flitting to different vantage points before vanishing, while horns sound for the last time.

Hall's film, like his stage production of the *Dream*, was a conscious attempt to get away from conventional representations associated with Mendelssohn's music and pre-Raphaelite art, which culminated in Reinhardt's stage productions and his film.[6] Like Brook immediately after him, Hall paid close attention to Shakespeare's text, but his film remained more representational and realistic than Brook's staging, which totally rejected the traditions Hall laments. Jan Kott directly influenced both directors, who recognized the erotic, sensual, and earthy aspects of human experience in *A Midsummer Night's Dream*, and who, in their different ways, tried to convey them. Both succeeded, at least for a time, in overthrowing the kind of theater and film associated with Reinhardt.

The most successful, most lavish film production after Hall's—Michael Hoffman's—waited thirty years to be produced. In the meantime, several other productions on film appeared, two of them for the smaller television screen, and one based on another RSC stage production, Adrian Noble's in 1994. As part of its series, *The Shakespeare Plays*, made expressly for television, the BBC produced *A Midsummer Night's Dream* in 1981, with Elijah Moshinsky as the director. Jonathan Miller was then the producer for the series, and in his view Shakespeare was basically a domestic playwright, a view that doubtless influenced this much less extravagant production of the *Dream* as well as several of the other plays Miller produced for the series. Therefore, the characters— even Oberon and Titania—behave more like ordinary people than they might otherwise. David Myerscough-Jones designed the production in seventeenth-century Cavalier style, and Stephen Oliver composed the unobstrusive but nonetheless superb incidental music.

Like Hall, Moshinsky merely trimmed Shakespeare's text, though he cut a good deal more of the last act, especially the courtiers' quips. The cast included Helen Mirren, now playing Titania against Peter McEnery's Oberon; Nigel Davenport as Theseus; Estelle Kohler as Hippolyta; Hugh Quarshie as Philostrate; Geoffrey Palmer as Quince; and Brian Glover as a somewhat subdued Bottom. Along with other principals, most of these players were, like those in Hall's film, experienced Shakespearean actors.

Since the production was made for television, many close- and mid-shots were used rather than the long ones that could encompass a large cast for the wider screen. Unfortunately, the production was somewhat inconsistent at times, revealing a lack of coherence, according to one critic. Hippolyta, for example, first seen wearing a courtly dress and pacing up and down like a caged tigress, shortly thereafter appears as "a bubbling enthusiastic fiancée."[7] The mechanicals speak in a variety of accents, from Cockney to northern England, set off from Quince's Home Counties speech and officiousness.

Moshinsky followed Hall in making the fairies, always a challenge for directors, a band of "lost" children, though a few of them, unlike Hall's, sport semitransparent wings. Helen Mirren's Titania appears with long blonde hair and a flowing white gown that recalls Anita Louise's Titania, but she is much sexier. Like Victor Jory in Reinhardt's film, McEnery's Oberon first appears on horseback, but there the comparison ends. McEnery wears an open shirt which, with his long dark hair, complements Titania's looks. This royal couple, hardly distinguished from the humans, is quite different from Hall's forest sprites. Puck, played by Phil Daniels, is a rather punk creature, bare chested except for a little ruff. If in some ways he resembles Reinhardt's elfin boy, he lacks Mickey Rooney's ebullience and Ian Holm's delight in mischief. Moshinsky's interpretation suggests that the two worlds, mortal and supernatural (or realistic and imaginary), are thus in close proximity, and the transition between them is neither so difficult nor so startling as one might suppose. Here, Peter Brook's influence may be operative.

The other production shown on television was produced in the summer of 1982 by Joseph Papp. It is essentially a filmed recording of a live performance at the Delacorte Theater in Central Park, New York. Intent on bringing Shakespeare to the people, Papp's New York Shakespeare Festival embodies several principles, such as free admission and multiethnic casts, which at the time of their inception were considered revolutionary. Except when adapting a play to a musical, as Papp did for *Two Gentlemen of Verona*, these productions rarely tamper with the text.[8] They often include Hollywood stars in the leads, and to make the productions as accessible as possible to everyone, actors avoid British accents, and contemporary or nearly contemporary sets and costumes are used. These are both kept quite simple since the Delacorte open-air stage does not permit elaborate settings.

Joseph Lapine directed Papp's *Dream* mainly for laughs, and audience response, recorded on the sound track, gives ample evidence of how enjoyable the performance was. The actors, too, seem to be having a good deal of fun, a little too much at times, perhaps, at the expense of the play's more serious preoccupations and psychological depths. Heidi Landesman's set design took full advantage of the park background. Theseus and Hippolyta, the four lovers and Egeus, the rude mechanicals, and the fairies all moved over the same lawns and hillocks, or through the same clumps of trees, but the stage is large enough to allow for one group to disappear into the woods as another comes on—much as they must have done on Shakespeare's stage. After all, one of Papp's principles was to recreate and convey as much as possible that earlier experience. Inevitably, there is a pond, but unlike Hall or Moshinsky—or Lepage later on—Lapine rarely had anyone splash around in it, and never during the lovers' quarrels. Emile Ardolino, the television director, min-gled long and mid-shots with close-ups very effectively. Most impressive is the opening sequence, which focuses on flowers or trees, giving the production a decidedly pastoral feel.

Some of the actors performed extremely well; others did not. Christine Baranski brought a new and appealing interpretation of Helena, playing her as the comedienne she really may be. Jeffrey DeMunn's Bottom is no Warwickshire yokel but a working-class New Yorker through and through, complete with baseball cap, sneakers, and accent. His part is broadly comic, like those of the other mechanicals, also New York blue-collar types. Bottom is a real ham but no prima donna, and his ham-miness projects a rather endearing quality. He is utterly uninhibited until almost the very end when, during Pyramus's death scene, he glimpses Titania watching from the shadows. Then his whole demeanor changes, and what was a robust and exuberant rendition becomes much quieter and more thoughtful—until the Bergomask restores jollity.

Steve Vinovitch's Quince, leading his singing band of thespians into the forest, is also very comical. Thisbe, played by a roly-poly young African American, Paul Bates, requires special prodding, literally, to raise his voice to the proper falsetto register. The fairies, male and fe-male, children and adults, provide their share of comedy as well. Some of the adults, even those playing Peaseblossom and Cobweb, appear wearing grotesque masks, horns, or grass skirts—as if they had just ar-rived from the South Sea islands or Africa.[9] The Indian boy is a small, black child who runs on stage at the beginning of 2.1 chased by fairies rather than following them. Michelle Shay's Titania, a handsome woman of color, wears a transparent body stocking covered at strategic places with sequins, not unlike Judi Dench's costume in Hall's film. Despite a tendency to croon, she speaks with great clarity, at times unfortunately bellowing her lines.

The worst casting and greatest disappointments are John Hurt's Oberon and Marcell Rosenblatt's Puck. Hurt simply cannot speak Shake-speare's verse properly, nor is he as mysterious and sinister as he intends; he is no Victor Jory. With Rosenblatt as Puck, Lapine revived the nineteenth-century tradition of casting a woman in the role, but the ex-periment here proves disastrous. Her Puck often comes running on stage shrieking or giggling hysterically. During Oberon's "fair vestal" speech in 2.1, she runs upstage to some shrubbery for no apparent reason, until at "Cupid's fiery shaft" (161) she launches a rocket, hardly a needed spectacle. Worse, returning with love-in-idleness, she runs on stage squealing with delight and directs a long, loud "raspberry" at the audience, who laugh more in surprise and embarrassment than out of genuine amusement. These and other similar incidents show how misguided some attempts at humor can be when performing so elegant a comedy as Shakespeare's *A Midsummer Night's Dream.*

Michael Hoffman's *A Midsummer Night's Dream* (1999) is in many ways the most spectacular and innovative film yet. Best seen on the large screen, it is available, like all the other major films, on videotape. Hoffman's lavishly illustrated book, with screenplay, introduction, and marginal notes, has been published.[10] Like Reinhardt, Hoffman used a number of Hollywood stars in his cast, including Michelle Pfeiffer as Titania, Stanley Tucci as Puck, Calista Flockhart as Helena, and Rupert Everett as Oberon. His most innovative conception was to cast Kevin Kline as Bottom and to set the production in nineteenth-century Tuscany.

Why the nineteenth century, and why Tuscany? As the promotional flyer distributed by Fox Searchlight Pictures and Regency Enterprises states,

> Amidst a sensuous and charming world of terraced hillsides and succulent culinary delights, Shakespeare's characters get a new comic lease on life as they explore their world on the new-fangled invention of the bicycle. Flying into the woods on two wheels, Tuscan nobles, actors and lovers find themselves at the mercy of mischievous sprites who rule the natural world.

The late Victorian age, moreover, as Hoffman says in the preface to his book, was a time when social convention was still a large part of everyday life. It was also a time when it still meant something to be an aristocrat. Besides, as he continues in his introduction, "there seemed no better visual metaphor for the representation of the Self than stiff collars, high necklines, tight corsets, and silly accessories."

As for transposing the location, Hoffman, who once lived in a Tuscan village, does not say much, but Tuscany and Greece are not very far apart, geographically and in other ways. It was a simple matter, then, to transfer Athens to Monte Athena, where Duke Theseus, a good-looking European aristocrat, lives in Villa Athena. His villa is actually the Palazzo Farnese, although the interiors were filmed at the Villa d'Este and the street scenes in Montepulciano. The production is a feast to the eyes, but it is also a banquet to the ears. Not only are the lines well spoken, though with American, not British accents, the music for the sound track is also excellent. Initially, however, it posed a problem for Hoffman. While setting the play at a later time and place had some distinct advantages and freed Hoffman from the "Hey Nonny Nonny" Elizabethan thing, he was at a loss to know what to use instead. When he learned that Tuscans listen to opera, "A door opened," he said. "Standing before me were Donizetti, Bellini, Verdi, the entire bel canto tradition. . . . In a moment several arias became integrated into the story."

But if one piece of the puzzle had fallen into place, Hoffman was still left with the question of how to provide music for the fairy scenes. He wanted "wit and beauty and mystery and magic and yearning and strangeness and romance and intelligence and sophistication and simplicity and sensibility and humour—And it can't get in the way of the dialogue, because, after all, it's Shakespeare." Simon Boswell, the composer, solved this problem for him. He combined ancient music with divergent popular traditions (Indian, Bulgarian, Syrian, and the like) with Mozart, Stravinsky, and Ravel, providing "a complex whole that had its own gorgeous and unique consistency."[11]

The film has other excellence as well. While some may have regarded casting Kevin Kline as Bottom a waste of the actor's fine talents, it turned out to be a brilliant decision. Originally scheduled to play Oberon, for whom he was more obviously suited, Kline reluctantly agreed to the new role. He actually conceived of a way to play Oberon, Theseus, *and* Bottom, according to Hoffman, noting that he was already seeing himself in the role of the grand ham who wants to play Thisbe, Lion, and all (Hoffman 1994, Introduction). Kline's Bottom was Bottom with a difference. When he first appears, he looks quite unlike his fellows, dressed in a dapper white suit, straw boater, colorful waistcoat, and a bow tie, for he fancies himself as a ladies' man—anything but a lowly weaver, although that is his trade. As Kline himself has said, Bottom "is an artist at heart. The urge to ally himself to ideas or representations of an heroic or transcendent nature is one of the defining principles of his character" (13).

Hoffman had further ideas, not all of them as inspired as these, perhaps. For instance, he endowed this Bottom with a shrewish wife.[12] She has no lines, at least in English, though she occasionally mutters in Italian. She appears briefly in conspicuous disapproval of her husband's behavior, both in the marketplace, where she first enters looking for him, and later in their small apartment. Again, Hoffman thought it would be a good idea, or at any rate funny, to have a couple of mischievous boys dump a load of donkey dung on Bottom as he finishes his speech in

"Ercles" vein at 1.2.33. In the film, the load turns into a wine flask full of Chianti, ruining Bottom's good (and only) suit and making him appear now as a poor, pitiful creature instead of a proud, ambitious thespian.

In Hoffman's interpretation, *A Midsummer Night's Dream* is Bottom's dream. "It wasn't Bottom the egotist, the clumsy outspoken braggart, nor Bottom the buffoon. It was Nick Bottom the dreamer, the actor, the pretender—Nick Bottom sitting at a café in a small Italian town dressed in a white suit, trying to look his best as a gentleman" (Hoffman 1994, Introduction). He clings to his delusions of grandeur because he has no love in his life. This conception led Hoffman to think of the love between Titania and Bottom as a real love story. In his interpretation, Bottom grows and changes through his experience in the forest, making him feel that perhaps, despite his unhappy marriage, he is truly lovable. It also made Titania "a woman who wanted to love simply and unconditionally, in a way that the politics of her relationship with Oberon made impossible."

As the film begins, Mendelssohn's music is heard while the credits roll and firefly lights dance around Villa Athena, Duke Theseus's grand Renaissance house. Peasant workers are preparing for a great feast. Servants hustle about, speaking Italian, setting out long tables for the expected guests. In the kitchen, cooks prepare tons of food. Overseeing all this activity is the duke, "winemaker, poet, hunter, warrior, statesman, lover, lord of all we've observed" (Hoffman 1994, Introduction), dressed appropriately in morning attire. When Theseus approaches Hippolyta, he puts his arms around her waist and hands her a rose. There is no suggestion of hostility between them; lines 11–19 about how he won her have been cut. They seem very much in love. Egeus enters and interrupts their kiss, and the action proper of the play begins.

In the controversy that ensues, Hippolyta is quietly appalled and turns away from Theseus when he summons Egeus and Demetrius to follow, leaving Lysander and Hermia alone to decide what to do. Throughout— good feminist that she is—Hippolyta sides with the young woman and offers what comfort she can. Once alone together, Lysander holds Hermia close and whispers his plan to elope, although the lines are cut and we do not hear him. Instead, the camera focuses on Demetrius watching Theseus and Egeus arguing over something, presumably the duke's attempt to get the old man to relent. A voice is heard from outside calling "Demetrius!" It is Helena, damp and bedraggled in the rain, holding her bicycle. Demetrius goes to the window, sees her, and closes the shutters.

Helena then begins her soliloquy (1.1.226–35) while walking her bike.

She passes Lysander and Hermia embracing. When they see her, Hermia calls to her, and they begin the dialogue, 180 ff., though a good portion of it is cut. Hermia assures her friend that Demetrius will no longer see her (202), and with a conspiratorial smile she leads Helena into a little grotto where Lysander relates their plan to elope (208–13). As the play-script indicates, the grotto is decorated with Bacchic figures: "a man and a woman, beautiful, exquisite bodies, adorned all in vines, grapes, and flowers. Between them is an odd fat little man who rides on the back of a turtle—creatures ancient and forgotten in this Victorian world" (Hoffman 1994, 7–8).

The scenes just described indicate how Hoffman altered Shakespeare's text to suit his purposes and decorated the film with suggestive paintings, sculptures, and statuary. His intention, however, was to complement the action and dialogue, not distract from it, although the lush landscape, architecture, and ornaments cannot help but interest the audience and compel their eyes. This becomes especially true of the forest scenes, where the fairies hold sway. In a marginal comment to the published screenplay, the designer, Luciana Arrighi, remarks,

> To express the fairy world, we turned to the Etruscans. The sets were based on the woods, tombs, and caves to which the Etruscans carried their dancing and feasting. This world was also related by a surreal quality in the locations, which were selected for heightened reality and the golds, russets, and orange colors of the designs. (Hoffman 1994, 20)

Hoffman further explains: "The choice of Italy led me to the Etruscans. Their interest in beauty, music, magic, divination, sensuality, their una-pologetic vanity, and their reverence for the feminine made them excel-lent models for the fairy world. This was especially true in contrast to the uptight, conventional world of the court" (21).

In the Fairy Bar, where 2.1 begins, elegant fairies and satyrs carouse together, and in a pond naked water nymphs play. Puck, little horns sprouting from either side of his head, appears drinking a beery sub-stance. He is older than usually cast; mostly bald, he has a fringe of grey hair. He greets a tired female fairy and offers her a seat near him (the playscript names her Cobweb, but otherwise we know her as First Fairy). Puck also offers her a drink, which she declines. At 32–34, Cobweb recognizes Puck as Robin Goodfellow and takes the offered drink after

Stanley Tucci as Puck and Rupert Everett as Oberon in Michael Hoffman's 1999 film. Courtesy of Photofest.

all, continuing the curtailed dialogue in which Puck admits to several pranks, a few of which the camera displays.

Puck and his fairy exit amidst thunder and lightning, arms around each other's drunken shoulders, when he suddenly pulls away to pee against a tree. Cobweb bids him farewell and points to a cliff face where figures dressed all in white are carrying a litter draped in silk: the Fairy Queen and her train. An earthquake shakes the ground as Puck announces that Oberon will hold sway there tonight. Titania's train does not heed Puck's warning to keep away, and the rumbling gets louder. A stroke of lightning illuminates Oberon on his throne, bare chested, his brows entwined with vine and laurel leaves and a horned crown upon his head. It is a spectacular entrance; the inspiration for Oberon was drawn directly from Gustav Moreau's painting of brooding Apollo in *The Muses Leaving Their Father Apollo* (Hoffman 1994, 25).

Oberon addresses Titania, speaking gently to her when she emerges from her tent-like covering: throughout the film, Everett downplays Oberon. Michelle Pfeiffer's Titania is stunningly beautiful; her long hair falls well below her waist, and her body is sprinkled over with sparkles. Near her is the little Indian prince. At her command—"Skip hence"— the fairies disappear as dancing firelights. As Oberon and Titania begin their quarrel, it pours rain, causing grapes and olives prematurely to fall—visible evidence of how their dispute has disrupted nature. Titania refuses Oberon's request to hand over the Indian boy, whose skin is the deep blue of the young god Krishna. Led forward on his pony, he is adorned in gold and canopied with flowers (Hoffman 1994, 25). Titania kisses him, and as she tells the sad story of his birth, her eyes fill with tears. When Oberon again asks her to give him up, she hisses at him. Oberon recoils and then sees Titania and her fairies high up on a cliff face, from where she speaks her last lines in the scene and disappears with her train.

This lavish cinematic display characterizes the fairy world. Meanwhile, with a good deal of noise, crashing, and whining, Demetrius and Helena enter on their bicycles. Demetrius tries to shoo Helena away, but she stays, honking her bicycle horn at him to keep his attention while he exasperatedly tries to fix a tire. Of the bikes and Helena's portrayal, Calista Flockhart pointed out, "She's not only obsessed with Demetrius, she's a little obsessed with her bike. It was a bit heavy, which was great, because it gave me an incredible obstacle to work with." Hoffman adds that the bike

> ends up symbolizing all the things she mythologizes about herself which make her a victim, like the idea that she is not pretty enough or good enough or lovable enough. It becomes the thing she carries around with her, like all the negative concepts of herself that she is eventually able to get rid of. (11)

Although Adrian Noble used a bicycle for Peter Quince in his production of the *Dream*, he made far less use of bicycles and their significance than Hoffman did in his film. Calista Flockhart, like Christine Baranski before her, shows in a different way what a comical figure Helena can be.

The comedy continues when Hermia and Lysander also enter the forest, riding their bikes, obviously tired and lost. Hermia wanders off to a partly secluded area to lie down. After she takes off some of her travel-worn clothes, Lysander creeps up to her and starts to fondle her breast. She kisses him but sends him farther off when his amorousness gets more intense. He is naked. The sexuality that these late Victorians try to repress asserts itself vigorously when the attraction becomes almost irresistible, as Hoffman indicates. Nevertheless, Hermia gently but firmly fends off Lysander. She tosses him a petticoat to wrap around his loins, and he finally lies down farther away from her.

As they sleep, Puck enters riding on a huge tortoise and spies Lysander asleep. He snoops around his bike, tries its horn, gets on it and rides over to Hermia, whom he pities. Then he rides back again to where Lysander lies and puts the love potion on his eyes. He obviously enjoys riding the newfangled vehicle. His mission accomplished, he rides off with Lysander's coat. Demetrius enters, followed by Helena, and disappears. Helena gives up, spots Lysander sleeping and puts her head on his chest to find out if he is alive or dead. When he awakens and declares his love for her, she becomes startled. His nakedness shocks her. She tosses him Hermia's petticoat, which he wraps around his loins (it is the only clothing he wears throughout the forest scenes), and runs off without her bike. Lysander grabs a bike and pedals off after her. Hermia awakens, frightened by her dream, and calls out to Lysander, who is no longer there.

These scenes demonstrate Hoffman's treatment of the young lovers in the forest, although they are only at the beginning of the trials and tribulations they endure. The comedy intensifies as later not only the men, but the women also come to blows. At one point, for example, when Helena tries to ride off on her bike, Lysander holds her back, and her rear wheel spins uselessly. In a rage, Hermia stamps on his bare foot with her boot, and he lets Helena go. When Helena rides off, she hits a bump and hurtles into a muddy pool. Far from sympathizing, Hermia now recognizes Helena as the cause of Lysander's defection. She begins her verbal attack, and soon the women grapple with each other in the mud, soon joined by Lysander and Demetrius, who vainly try to rescue Helena. All four now grapple in the primordial element, reminiscent of Lepage's production and with much the same significance.

The mechanicals contribute to the comedy in their way, too, once they enter the forest to rehearse their play. When Bottom retires "backstage" awaiting his cue, he finds a walking stick and a top hat that he cannot resist trying on. As he gazes at himself admiringly in a pool of water, his narcissism links him to that of the fairies and helps prepare for what comes next. Returning to the rehearsal stage, he takes off his hat, and the others become frightened by his transformation—huge, furry ears sprouting from his head, and hair covering his face. Left alone, Bottom sings and hee-haws to keep up his courage and in so doing awakens Titania who is lying in her hammock above him.

The Fairy Queen begins ardently wooing Bottom, much to his amazement. He jokes with her about the nature of love, but when he tries to escape from her advances, she causes the vines and plants around him to turn into snaky ropes, twine about his feet, and hoist him upside down. At her signal, a fairy in the treetops cuts the ropes, and he drops onto Titania's hammock, where she resumes her adoration more enthusiastically than ever. Putting her arms around his head and caressing his ears, Titania explains who and what she is and how much she loves him. Her sexuality, like that of the other forest creatures, is far less inhibited than that of the mortals. She summons Mustardseed, Peaseblossom, and the rest, who appear as winged young girls offering them food and drink. A veritable fête champêtre ensues, in which many forest inhabitants participate. Opera music plays in the background, and some wood nymphs flirt with the satyrs. Under the influence of all the wine and wonder, Bottom begins to fall in love with this beautiful queen, who orders her retinue to attend on him lavishly. Chanting "Hail, mortal!" the assembled company applauds as Titania places a crown of golden leaves on Bottom's head and their amorousness burgeons.

Lying on the ground wondering what is happening to Titania, Oberon receives the news from Puck, and, unencumbered by Victorian morals, both laugh. Eventually, of course, Oberon takes pity on his queen, and they are reconciled. So, too, are the young lovers after Oberon scolds Puck for causing his mischief, pulling him by the ear and ordering him to make everything right, as the couples emerge from the pool and chase each other away. Puck rides his bike, trailing a huge cloud of fog behind him, and finds the men desperately trying to locate one another in the fog. After becoming still more confused, thanks to Puck's invisible tauntings, they fall asleep on the ground, followed by Hermia and then Helena, crawling through the brush, mud caked on her face and arms. They are soon lying fast asleep, their bicycles suspended above ground with the wheels spinning, as if to suck the fog back into the saddle bags. Thanks to Puck's intervention, the couples now lie side by side in the proper order.

Day breaks. As the sun rises above the horizon, a formal hunt gathers near Theseus's palazzo. Theseus and Hippolyta ride off on horseback with the others (she rides sidesaddle) as a team of beaters thrash through the woods. A wild boar runs frantically around trying to avoid the hounds hot in pursuit, reflecting perhaps the earlier chases we have witnessed. Theseus and Hippolyta dismount and walk up a hill, where they find the young couples asleep and, like Adam and Eve, naked except for some leaves covering their vital parts. Their freshly laundered clothes lie be-

side them along with their pristine bicycles. Called on to explain how
they came there, Lysander gives his account, which in no way pleases
Egeus, who has come upon them, too. Demetrius interposes, professing
his love now for Helena. Theseus and Hippolyta confer apart and, probably under his bride's influence, the duke delivers his decision, overriding Egeus's concerns. The couples kiss happily, as the scene ends.

In the final scene, an orchestra plays music from *La Traviata* on the
palazzo grounds. The lilting tunes here as elsewhere in the film do not
connect with the tragic outcome of the opera but hint, like the performance of "Pyramus and Thisbe" later, of what might have been. In the
formal garden the feast winds down, the guests dressed in their finery
and the married couples in their wedding garments looking very handsome indeed. Egeus, the only one who looks discontented, sulks at his
place. Theseus delivers his speech on the imagination, while the camera
focuses appropriately on the young couples. Lines 7–17 in 5.1 have been
omitted—the association of the lover and the lunatic, after what has just
been shown, might be too close for comfort at this moment of joy, adding
a further discordant note amidst all the revelry: Egeus's behavior is suf-
ficient.

Philostrate delivers the "menu" of possible entertainments to Theseus,
who reads it aloud, voice over, while the camera pans across groups of
hopeful performers. They are a varied bunch of hopefuls. Much to the
outraged disappointment of Master Antonio and his "company of prigs"
in short Roman tunics, who have been practicing "a kind of stilted but
well-rehearsed dramatic reading" (Hoffman 1994, 95), Theseus selects
Quince's play as the evening's entertainment. The scene shifts to the
indoor theater, where all the seats are filled except for those in the ducal
box. Lines 84–105 have been cut. Instead, the camera shows the actors
backstage nervously preparing to go on and praying together to the
strains of Schubert's "Ave Maria." Then Mendelssohn's "Wedding
March" sounds and, speaking lines 82–83, Theseus enters with his duchess and the other two couples to general applause.

Omitting the prologue on which he has labored so hard (and the banter
it arouses in the original text, 5.1.108–25), Quince introduces the cast,
who comically mime their parts. The mechanicals perform "Pyramus and
Thisbe" with a good deal of slapstick, most of it unintended. It includes,
for example, a fracas involving Moonshine's dog, who takes one end of
Thisbe's scarf in his mouth as he and Bottom engage in a tug of war.
The dog loses his grip and lands in the arms of a startled Philostrate,
who is standing behind Theseus. Pyramus's death throes win applause,

though Quince has to prompt him to say "devoured" instead of "deflow-ered" (276, a correction Hoffman introduced rather than Shakespeare). Flute, as Thisbe, begins his long speech in a high falsetto voice but quickly drops it at line 308 and continues in normal tones. At 320 Flute takes off his wig too, for, reminiscent of Hall's film, he is nearly over-come by the seriousness of the situation and real tears fill his eyes.

Quince, we see, is similarly affected; the stage audience also becomes hushed by the action before them, for what has begun so farcically has now turned to tragedy. At 5.1.329, the end of Thisbe's monologue, si-lence follows for several long moments, until the audience, including even Bottom, breaks into loud applause. The show has ended; at The-seus's behest neither epilogue nor Bergomask follows. Instead, Philos-trate delivers a note to Peter Quince from Theseus after they exit. When Quince reads "Very notably discharged," the troupe fall over themselves in hugs and kisses at their success. This incident replaces 337–38, 343–78.

The couples ascend the staircase at Theseus's command, "Lovers, to bed" (5.1.342), kissing and hugging each other as they go. Servants ex-tinguish the hall lights, and all is silent, as strains of the intermezzo from Mascagni's *Cavalleria Rusticana* are heard. Sparkles appear. Oberon speaks (voice-over) lines 369 and 379–86 (387–94 are cut), as the camera focuses on Lysander and Hermia, Helena and Demetrius, naked in their beds, making love. Theseus and Hippolyta, still clothed, are in their own room, dancing happily together. At line 399, Theseus lifts Hippolyta and carries her, laughing, to bed.

Sparkles aplenty now dance along hallways and up the rotunda of the palazzo. Oberon summons all the fairies away, and the scene shifts to the piazza outside, where Quince & Co. are drinking and cheering each other on, bidding each other goodnight. As the company departs, a sweeper enters with his broom, pauses a moment, and takes off his hat, revealing Puck, who delivers his epilogue. At 5.1.413 the camera switches to Bottom in his room who is putting away his white suit, marveling at the tiny ring he has found in his pocket. After blowing out his candle, he watches the sparkles outside his window. He gazes in wonder as the lights ascend and meld into stars, making it clear that this is his dream above all others. Puck delivers the last lines of his epilogue, hoists his broom onto his shoulder, and walks off to strains of music. The film's credits roll as the camera pans over the sleeping town, and the music changes to the waltz from *La Traviata*.

The many splendors of this production notwithstanding, many critics found faults with it. MacDonald Jackson's far more generous and thoughtful essay on Hoffman's film appeared in the *Shakespeare Newsletter*.[13] At the outset he recognizes the complexities of Shakespeare's play and reviews a number of previous directorial attempts to deal with them, including the Reinhardt-Dieterle film and Adrian Noble's. Unlike other reviewers, Jackson does not dismiss Hoffman's innovations; instead, he finds much to admire in them. "The sheer beauty of the *mise en scène*, natural and architectural," he asserts, "is itself entrancing. The young women, moreover, look gorgeous in their Victorian lace collars, long floating dresses, and flower-bedecked hats" (1999, 37). More than any other critic, Jackson recognized but did not belittle Hoffman's debts to the art of the Renaissance and to that of other periods; he praised, for example, the imitations of John Waterhouse's "Hylas and the Nymphs" and Gustav Moreau's *The Muses Leaving Their Father Apollo*. Furthermore, "Hoffman's Etruscan substrata catches very well the play's concern with death and the numinous."

Jackson's analysis of the acting is similarly perceptive. In an acute observation, he notes that in this film Oberon's despicable trick on Titania "opens his own eyes" to what he has done, to his real love for his queen, and to what he may still regain. Jackson recognizes without disparagement that "the relationship between Bottom and the Fairy Queen [is] at the heart of this film" (1999, 38). Withal, "Hoffman is expert at shuttling between the actual and the envisioned." Jackson concludes that, unlike many modern theater productions, which "undercut the endings with silences, ironies, and resentments," Hoffman's movie is "truer to the spirit of Shakespeare's popular, romantic art." It "gets the essentials right, capturing the play's emotional richness, emphasizing its movement from discord to harmony, conveying its lyricism in cinematic terms, and fully exploring its concern with the transforming power of the imagination" (44). That is a judgment with which many may concur.

NOTES

1. See Jack Jorgens, *Shakespeare on Film*. Bloomington: Indiana University Press, 1977, 41.

2. Samuel Crowl, *Shakespeare Observed: Studies in Performance on Stage and Screen*. Athens: University of Ohio Press, 1992, 67.

3. John Collick, *Shakespeare, Cinema and Society*. Manchester, England: Manchester University Press, 1989, 90.

4. Roger Manvell, *Theater and Film*. Cranbury, N.J.: Associated University Presses, 1979, 168.

5. Crowl, *Shakespeare Observed*, 73.

6. Manvell, *Theater and Film*, 123. See also Kenneth S. Rothwell, *A History of Shakespeare on Screen*. Cambridge, England: Cambridge University Press, 1999, 147–49.

7. Nicholas Shrimpton, "Hot Ice and Wondrous Strange Snow," *Times Literary Supplement*, December 25, 1981. Reprinted in *Shakespeare on Television*, ed. James Bulman and Herbert Coursen, 283. Hanover, N.H.: University Press of New England, 1988.

8. The only exception in the production of the *Dream* was the omission of Theseus's speech on the imagination at the beginning of act 5 and Hippolyta's response.

9. Papp and Lapine intended to present examples of fairies and folklore from a variety of cultures and myths. See Arthur Ganz, "Shakespeare in New York City," *Shakespeare Quarterly* 34 (1983), 106.

10. Michael Hoffman, adapter. *William Shakespeare's A Midsummer Night's Dream*. New York: Harper Entertainment, 1999. The book is unfortunately now out of print but available through libraries.

11. The information in this paragraph may be found in the film's Web site <http://foxsearchlight.com/midfinal/html/conservatory>.

12. Russell Jackson notes that this idea was first considered but then dropped for the Reinhardt-Dieterle film. See his article in *Shakespeare Bulletin* 16 (Fall 1998), 40.

13. MacDonald P. Jackson, " 'A Wood Near Monte Athena': Michael Hoffman's *A Midsummer Night's Dream*," *Shakespeare Newsletter* 49 (Summer 1999), 29, 37–38, 44, 48.

SELECTED BIBLIOGRAPHY

BIBLIOGRAPHY

Carroll, D. Allen, and Gary Jay Williams, eds. *A Midsummer Night's Dream: An Annotated Bibliography*. New York: Garland, 1986. The most extensive and useful annotated bibliography up to the date of publication.

EDITIONS

Berger, Tom. *A Midsummer Night's Dream, 1600*. The Malone Society Reprints, vol. 157. New York: Oxford University Press, 1995. Not strictly an edition but a facsimile reprint of the first quarto, with a brief textual introduction.

Brooks, Harold, ed. *A Midsummer Night's Dream*. Arden Shakespeare 2. London: Methuen, 1979. A very full introduction (163 pages), collation, and notes.

Foakes, R. A., ed. *A Midsummer Night's Dream*. New Cambridge Shakespeare. Cambridge, England: Cambridge University Press, 1984. Full introduction, collation, and commentary, with reading list but no index.

Holland, Peter, ed. *A Midsummer Night's Dream*. Oxford Shakespeare. Oxford: Clarendon Press, 1994. Full introduction, collation, and commentary. Indexed, but no reading list.

Quiller-Couch, Arthur, and John Dover Wilson, eds. *A Midsummer Night's Dream*. The New Shakespeare. Cambridge, England: Cambridge University Press, 1924. The introduction is written by Quiller-Couch; the text and commentary, including textual notes, are contributed by Wilson.

TEXTUAL STUDIES

Greg, W. W. *The Shakespeare First Folio.* Oxford: Clarendon Press, 1955 (1962). Still a very sound compendium of facts and interpretation.

Hinman, Charlton. *The Printing and Proof Reading of the First Folio of Shakespeare.* 2 vols. Oxford: Clarendon Press, 1963. The pioneering work on the subject.

Ioppolo, Grace. *Revising Shakespeare.* Cambridge, Mass.: Harvard University Press, 1991. An excellent study of all the plays that Shakespeare apparently revised, giving specific examples and the evidence underlying this theory.

Lull, Janis. "Textual Theory, Literary Interpretation, and the Last Act of *A Midsummer Night's Dream.*" In *"A Midsummer Night's Dream": Critical Essays,* edited by Dorothea Kehler, 241–58. New York: Garland, 1998. The additions and alterations in Theseus's speeches in act 5 show his evolution from "from rationalist to imaginationist."

Turner, Robert K. "Printing Methods and Textual Problems in *A Midsummer Night's Dream,* Q1." *Studies in Bibliography* 15 (1962): 33–55.

Wells, Stanley, and Gary Taylor, with John Jowett and William Montgomery. *William Shakespeare: A Textual Companion.* Oxford: Clarendon Press, 1987. Contains textual analyses of all the plays as well as collations and textual notes.

SOURCES AND CONTEXTS

Andrews, John F., ed. *William Shakespeare: His World, His Work, His Influence.* 3 vols. New York: Charles Scribner's Sons, 1985. Volume I contains many essays on Shakespeare's "world" (e.g., government and politics under Elizabeth I and James I, law and legal institutions, economic life, manners, dress, and decorum).

Briggs, K. M. *The Anatomy of Puck: An Examination of Fairy Beliefs Among Shakespeare's Contemporaries and Successors.* London: Routledge and Kegan Paul, 1959. Exactly what the subtitle indicates.

Bullough, Geoffrey. *Narrative and Dramatic Sources of Shakespeare's Plays.* 8 vols. New York: Columbia University Press, 1957–75. The standard and most complete reference work for the sources of Shakespeare's plays.

Chambers, E. K. *William Shakespeare.* 2 vols. Oxford: Clarendon Press, 1930. Provides much useful information on the contexts of the plays.

Garber, Marjorie. *Dream in Shakespeare.* New Haven, Conn.: Yale University Press, 1974. An excellent analysis of Shakespeare's use of dreams and the theories that underlie many of them.

Holmer, Joan Ozark. "No 'Vain Fantasy': Shakespeare's Refashioning of Nashe for Dreams and Queen Mab." In *"Romeo and Juliet": Texts, Contexts, and Interpretation*, edited by Jay L. Halio, 49–82. Newark: University of Delaware Press, 1995. Demonstrates Shakespeare's debt to Thomas Nashe and John Lyly's earlier use of diminutive fairies.

Latham, Minor White. *The Elizabethan Fairies*. New York: Columbia University Press, 1930. A study of Elizabethan knowledge and representation of fairies in various works.

Paster, Gail Kern, and Skiles Howard. *A Midsummer Night's Dream: Texts and Contexts*. Boston: Bedford/St. Martin's, 1999. Contains the text of the play and many excerpts regarding its intellectual and social contexts.

Rose, Carol. *Spirits, Fairies, Leprechauns, and Goblins: An Encyclopedia*. New York: W. W. Norton, 1996. A useful and up-to-date compendium of information on the subject.

Wells, Stanley. "*A Midsummer Night's Dream* Revisited." *Critical Survey* 3 (1991): 14–29. Rejects the theory that the play was written for a wedding in some noble family.

Woodbridge, Linda. *Women and the English Renaissance*. Urbana: University of Illinois Press, 1984. Especially good on female friendships.

GENERAL CRITICISM

Barber, C. L. *Shakespeare's Festive Comedy*. Princeton, N.J.: Princeton University Press, 1959. A groundbreaking study of the nature of Shakespearean comedy, with a fine chapter on the *Dream*.

Berry, Ralph. *Shakespeare's Comedies*. Princeton, N.J.: Princeton University Press, 1972. His chapter "The Dream and the Play," 89–110, treats the baroque aspects of *A Midsummer Night's Dream*.

Brown, John Russell. "Love's Truth and the Judgements of *A Midsummer Night's Dream* and *Much Ado About Nothing*." In *Shakespeare and His Comedies*, 82–123. 2d ed. London: Methuen, 1962. Emphasizes the irrationality of love's choices in the former.

Charlton, H. B. *Shakespearian Comedy*. London: Methuen, 1938. The chapter on *A Midsummer Night's Dream*, 100–122, relates it to Shakespeare's earlier comedies and treats the various "worlds" of the play.

Clayton, Tom. " 'So Bright Things Come to Confusion'; or, What Else Is *A Midsummer Night's Dream* About?" In *Shakespeare: Text and Theater: Essays in Honor of Jay L. Halio*, edited by Lois Potter and Arthur F. Kinney, 62–91. Newark: University of Delaware Press, 1999. Wide ranging essays that cover numerous topics, including an important account of the Indian boy and the question of "flower power."

Dent, R. W. "Imagination in *A Midsummer Night's Dream*." *Shakespeare Quarterly* 15 (1964): 115–29. Reprinted in *"A Midsummer Night's Dream": Critical Essays*, edited by Dorothea Kehler, 85–106. New York: Garland,

1998. A thorough examination of imagination and the way it works in this play.

Evans, Bertrand. *Shakespeare's Comedies*. Oxford: Clarendon Press, 1960. Discusses "discrepancy awareness" in the comedies and links *A Midsummer Night's Dream* to *The Merchant of Venice* in the second chapter: "All Shall Be Well: The Way Found."

Kehler, Dorothea, ed. *"A Midsummer Night's Dream": Critical Essays*. New York: Garland, 1998. Contains many important and informative essays.

Kott, Jan. *Shakespeare Our Contemporary*. Translated by Boleslaw Taborski. 2d. ed. London: Methuen, 1967. The chapter on *A Midsummer Night's Dream*, "Titania and the Ass's Head," 207–28, emphasizes the erotic aspects of the play and has significantly influenced modern productions, such as Peter Brook's.

Leggatt, Alexander. *Shakespeare's Comedy of Love*. London: Methuen, 1974. Excellent discussions of Shakespeare's romantic comedies.

McFarland, Thomas. *Shakespeare's Pastoral Comedy*. Chapel Hill: University of North Carolina Press, 1972. McFarland's chapter on *A Midsummer Night's Dream* disputes Jan Kott's contention about the play's eroticism.

Ornstein, Robert. *Shakespeare's Comedies*. Newark: University of Delaware Press, 1986. Covers all the comedies in jargon-free, lucidly written language with many fine insights.

Patterson, Annabel. "Bottom's Up: Festive Theory in *A Midsummer Night's Dream*." In *"A Midsummer Night's Dream": Critical Essays*, edited by Dorothea Kehler, 165–78. New York: Garland, 1998. A good supplement to C. L. Barber's chapter on the play.

Schanzer, Ernest. "*A Midsummer Night's Dream*." In *Shakespeare: The Comedies*, edited by Kenneth Muir, 26–31. Englewood Cliffs, N.J.: Prentice-Hall, 1965. Concerns the theme of love-madness in the play.

Young, David P. *Something of Great Constancy: The Art of "A Midsummer Night's Dream."* New Haven, Conn.: Yale University Press, 1966. One of the best books devoted entirely to the play.

PSYCHOANALYTICAL CRITICISM

Aronson, Alex. *Psyche and Symbol in Shakespeare*. Bloomington: Indiana University Press, 1972. Contains a Jungian analysis of the *Dream*. Especially good on the forest symbolism and Puck.

Faber, Melvin D. "Hermia's Dream: Royal Road to *A Midsummer Night's Dream*." *Literature and Psychology* 22 (1972): 179–90. Hermia's dream fulfills her wish for sex with Lysander.

Garber, Marjorie. *Dream in Shakespeare*. New Haven, Conn.: Yale University Press, 1974. The chapter on *A Midsummer Night's Dream*, "Spirits of

Another Sort," 59–87, focuses on the play's ambiguities or double meanings.

Gui, Weston A. "Bottom's Dream." *American Imago* 9 (1952–53): 251–305. Bottom's dream is the key dream in the play and is very "motherly."

Holland, Norman N. "Hermia's Dream." In *Representing Shakespeare*, edited by Murray M. Schwartz and Coppélia Kahn, 1–20. Baltimore: Johns Hopkins University Press, 1980. Concerns the three phases of psychoanalytical criticism, with specific reference to interpretations of Hermia's dream, including Holland's own admittedly subjective and personal analysis.

―――. *Psychoanalysis and Shakespeare*. New York: McGraw-Hill, 1966. Still an invaluable reference for psychoanalytical studies up to its date of publication.

Jacobson, Donald F. "A Note on Shakespeare's *A Midsummer Night's Dream*." *American Imago* 19 (1962): 21–26. Women must surrender oedipal wishes to mature.

Kaplan, Morton. "*The American Imago* in Retrospect: An Article-Review." *Literature and Psychology* 13 (1963): 112–16. A critique of earlier essays and a comment on the play's adaptive mechanism (regression in the wood to childhood memories).

Lindsay, Jack. "Shakespeare and Tom Thumb." *Life and Letters* 58 (1948): 119–27. Concerns the sexual implications of the fairies' reduced size.

GENDER CRITICISM

Bamber, Linda. *Comic Women, Tragic Men: A Study of Gender and Genre in Shakespeare*. Stanford, Calif.: Stanford University Press, 1982. A very sensible approach to gender criticism of Shakespeare.

Desmet, Christy. "Disfiguring Women with Masculine Tropes: A Rhetorical Reading of *A Midsummer Night's Dream*." In *"A Midsummer Night's Dream": Critical Essays*, edited by Dorothea Kehler, 299–329. New York: Garland, 1998. Concerns Theseus's speech to Hermia about marriage and celibacy.

Dusinberre, Juliet. *Shakespeare and the Nature of Women*. 2d ed. New York: St. Martin's Press, 1996. The preface to the second edition, published twenty years after the first, surveys the development of gender criticism.

Garner, Shirley Nelson. "*A Midsummer Night's Dream*: 'Jack Shall Have Jill; / Naught Shall Go Ill.' " *Women's Studies* 9 (1981): 47–63. Reprinted in *"A Midsummer Night's Dream": Critical Essays*, edited by Dorothea Kehler, 127–43. New York: Garland, 1998. The play moves toward satisfying men's needs at the expense of women's bonds with each other.

Gohlke, Madelon. " 'I Wooed Thee with My Sword': Shakespeare's Tragic Paradigm." In *Representing Shakespeare*, edited by Murray M. Schwartz and Coppélia Kahn, 170–87. Baltimore: Johns Hopkins University Press, 1980. Concerns the relationship between psychoanalytical and feminist criticism.

Hackett, Helen. *William Shakespeare: "A Midsummer Night's Dream."* Plymouth, England: Northcote House, 1997. Contains a chapter on "The Play in Its Time: Female Power," which discusses, among other things, mentioned but absent mothers in the play.

Lenz, Carolyn Ruth Swift, Gayle Greene, and Carol Thomas Neely, eds. *The Woman's Part: Feminist Criticism of Shakespeare*. Urbana: University of Illinois Press, 1980. An early but still useful collection of feminist essays. Madelon Gohlke's essay first appeared here.

Traub, Valerie. "The (In)significance of 'Lesbian' Desire in Early Modern England." In *Erotic Politics: Desire on the Renaissance Stage*, edited by Susan Zimmerman, 150–69. New York: Routledge, 1992. Discusses the eradication of homoerotic desire among women in the play.

NEW HISTORICISM AND CULTURAL MATERIALISM

Hawkes, Terence. "Or." In *New Casebooks: "A Midsummer Night's Dream,"* edited by Richard Dutton, 223–58. New York: St. Martin's Press, 1996. An interesting discussion of the name "Nedar" and its significance in the *Dream*, as well as several other aspects of the play, including parenthood.

———. *William Shakespeare: "King Lear."* Plymouth, England: Northcote House, 1995. Although he focuses mainly on *King Lear*, Hawkes gives a good account of both New Historicism and Cultural Materialism.

Hendricks, Margo. " 'Obscured by Dreams': Race, Empire, and Shakespeare's *A Midsummer Night's Dream*." *Shakespeare Quarterly* 47 (1996): 37–60. A postcolonial treatment of the Indian boy and the struggle for possession of him.

Leinwand, Theodore B. " 'I Believe We Must Leave the Killing Out': Deference and Accommodation in *A Midsummer Night's Dream*." In *"A Midsummer Night's Dream": Critical Essays*, edited by Dorothea Kehler, 145–61. New York: Garland, 1998. Originally published in *Renaissance Papers 1986*, edited by Dale B. J. Randall and Joseph Porter, 11–30. Durham, N.C.: Southeastern Renaissance Conference, 1986. On Shakespeare's concern with the strategies of accommodation in performances before nobility.

McDonald, Marcia. "Bottom's Space: Historicizing Comic Theory and Practice in *A Midsummer Night's Dream*." In *Acting Funny: Comic Theory and Practice in Shakespeare's Plays*, edited by Frances Teague, 85–108. Rutherford, N.J.: Fairleigh Dickinson Press, 1994. Concerns the debate over the function of the stage in Shakespeare's time.

Montrose, Louis Adrian. "*A Midsummer Night's Dream* and the Shaping Fantasies of Elizabethan Culture: Gender, Power, Form." In *Rewriting the Renaissance: The Discourses of Sexual Difference in Early Modern Europe*, edited by Margaret W. Ferguson, Maureen Quilligan, and Nancy J. Vickers, 65–87. Chicago: University of Chicago Press, 1986. A longer and more extensively documented version of the essay which first appeared in *Representations* (Spring 1983): 61–94.

Schneider, Michael. "Bottom's Dream, the Lion's Roar, and Hostility of Class Difference in *A Midsummer Night's Dream*." In *From the Bard to Broadway*, edited by Karelisa V. Hartigan, 191–212. Lanham, Md.: University Press of America, 1987. A classical Marxist interpretation of the play.

MYTH AND ARCHETYPAL CRITICISM

Barber C. L. *Shakespeare's Festive Comedy: A Study of Dramatic Form and Its Relation to Social Custom*. Princeton, N.J.: Princeton University Press, 1959. A landmark study of Shakespeare's "saturnalian" comedy. The chapter on the *Dream* includes a discussion of the ritual of May games.

Berry, Edward. *Shakespeare's Comic Rites*. Cambridge, England: Cambridge University Press, 1984. Focuses on the rites of passage in the comedies.

Frye, Northrop. "Archetypal Criticism: Theory of Myths." In *Anatomy of Criticism*, 131–239. Princeton, N.J.: Princeton University Press, 1957. A standard work that defines archetypal criticism and the patterns of myth in literature.

———. *A Natural Perspective*. New York: Columbia University Press, 1965. On Shakespearean comedy, with several specific references to *A Midsummer Night's Dream*.

Girard, René. *Theater of Envy: William Shakespeare*. New York: Oxford University Press, 1991. Contains several perceptive essays on the *Dream*, including one on ritual sacrifice that involves Puck.

PERFORMANCE CRITICISM AND STAGE HISTORY

Bentley, G. E. *Jacobean and Caroline Drama*. 5 vols. Oxford: Oxford University Press, 1941–68. Continues the history of drama where E. K. Chambers leaves off in *The Elizabethan Stage*.

Berry, Ralph. *On Directing Shakespeare*. 2d ed. London: Hamish Hamilton, 1989. Contains an enlightening interview with Peter Brook on his production of the *Dream*.

Brown, John Russell. *Free Shakespeare*. London: Heinemann, 1974. Brown advocates giving actors more freedom as against freezing productions according to the director's "concept." Contains his review of Peter Brook's *Dream*.

Bulman, James, and Herbert Coursen, eds. *Shakespeare on Television*. Hanover,

N.H.: University Press of New England, 1988. Contains an excellent review by Nicholas Shrimpton of the BBC-TV *Dream*.

Chambers, E. K. *The Elizabethan Stage*. 4 vols. Oxford: Clarendon Press, 1924. Still a very useful reference work.

―――. *William Shakespeare*. 2 vols. Oxford: Clarendon Press, 1930. Valuable information on Shakespeare's theatrical life.

Crowl, Samuel. *Shakespeare Observed: Studies in Performance on Stage and Screen*. Athens: University of Ohio Press, 1992. Crowl is a very perceptive theater and film critic.

Geckle, George L. "Lepage's *Dream*." *Shakespeare Bulletin* 11 (1993): 27. A perceptive review of Lepage's production.

Gelb, Arthur. "Shakespeare Rides the Range in Texan 'Dream.' " *New York Times*, April 1, 1959, 44. A review of the "Western style" *Dream* directed by Alex Reeves.

Halio, Jay L. *Shakespeare in Performance: A Midsummer Night's Dream*. 2d ed. Manchester, England: Manchester University Press, 2003. Surveys the earlier history of the play in performance and analyzes in detail a number of the most important twentieth-century stage and film productions, especially Peter Brook's.

Hamburger, Maik. "New Concepts in Staging *A Midsummer Night's Dream*." *Shakespeare Survey* 40 (1988): 51–61. Discusses German productions of the *Dream* in the latter part of the twentieth century.

Hogan, Charles B. *Shakespeare in the Theatre, 1701–1800*. 2 vols. Oxford: Oxford University Press, 1957. A standard reference work for eighteenth-century productions.

King, T. J. *Casting Shakespeare's Plays*. Cambridge, England: Cambridge University Press, 1992. A survey of roles as performed by Shakespeare's company.

Jackson, MacDonald P. " 'A Wood Near Monte Athena': Michael Hoffman's *A Midsummer Night's Dream*." *Shakespeare Newsletter* 49 (Summer 1999): 29, 37–38, 44, 48. The best review of Michael Hoffman's film, it identifies much of the music and other artistic effects.

Jorgens, Jack. *Shakespeare on Film*. Bloomington: Indiana University Press, 1977. One of the first books on Shakespeare on film and one of the best.

Kisselgoff, Anna. "On Wings of Mendelssohn and Shakespeare." *New York Times*, February 13, 1993, 11. Concerns the revival of Balanchine's ballet.

Linzer, Martin. "*A Midsummer Night's Dream* in East Germany." Translated by Brigitte Kueppers. *Drama Review* 25 (1981): 45–54.

Loney, Glen. *Peter Brook's Production of William Shakespeare's "A Midsummer Night's Dream" for the Royal Shakespeare Company: The Complete and Authorized Acting Edition*. Stratford-upon-Avon, England: Royal Shakespeare Company, 1974.

Manvell, Roger. *Theater and Film.* Cranbury, N.J.: Associated University Presses, 1979. A very useful guide for the period covered.

Morley, Henry. *Journal of a London Playgoer, from 1851 to 1866.* London, 1891. An astute account of stage productions in the mid-nineteenth century.

Odell, George C. *Annals of the New York Stage.* 15 vols. New York: Columbia University Press, 1927–49. A very extensive and useful compendium of facts for Shakespearean productions as well as others.

―――. *Shakespeare from Betterton to Irving.* 2 vols. New York: Scribner's, 1920. An early but still very informative stage history.

Ringler, William. "The Number of Actors in Shakespeare's Early Plays." In *The Seventeenth-Century Stage*, edited by G. E. Bentley, 110–34. Chicago: University of Chicago Press, 1968. A good account of the way in which roles were probably doubled in Shakespeare's plays.

Rothwell, Kenneth S. *A History of Shakespeare on Screen.* Cambridge, England: Cambridge University Press, 1999. A standard history of the subject, with a useful filmography at the end.

Salgado, Gamani. *Eyewitnesses of Shakespeare.* New York: Barnes and Noble, 1975. Contains some illuminating excerpts of criticisms from those who actually saw the plays performed.

Selbourne, David. *The Making of "A Midsummer Night's Dream."* London: Methuen, 1982. Concerns Peter Brook's RSC production of 1970.

Shattuck, Charles. *Shakespeare on the American Stage: From the Hallams to Edwin Booth.* Washington, D.C.: Folger Books, 1976. This is the first of two volumes on stage productions of Shakespeare's plays in America. Well illustrated.

Shaw, George Bernard. *Dramatic Opinions and Essays.* 2 vols. London: Constable, 1906. Contains reviews and critiques of Shakespeare productions as well as others. Shaw was a very astute but sometimes severe critic of Shakespeare.

Speaight, Robert. *Shakespeare on the Stage.* Boston: Little, Brown, 1973. Well written and well illustrated. Covers foreign productions along with English-language ones.

Stone, George Winchester. "*A Midsummer Night's Dream* in the Hands of Garrick and Colman." *PMLA* 54 (1939): 467–82. A good description of the adaptation in the eighteenth century.

Styan, John L. *The Shakespeare Revolution.* Cambridge, England: Cambridge University Press, 1977. Discusses changes that occurred in Shakespearean representations during the twentieth century.

Summers, Montague. *The Restoration Theatre.* New York: Macmillan, 1934. An early but useful stage history for the period.

Trewin, J. C. *Shakespeare on the English Stage, 1900–1964.* London: Barrie and Rockliff, 1964. Published in the centennial year, with many eye-witness accounts of productions.

Watkins, Ronald, and Jeremy Lemmon. *In Shakespeare's Playhouse: "A Midsummer Night's Dream."* Totowa, N.J.: Humanities Press, 1974. Describes how the play was performed at the Globe.

Williams, Gary Jay. *Our Moonlight Revels: "A Midsummer Night's Dream" in the Theatre.* Iowa City: University of Iowa Press, 1997. The fullest account of the play's stage history up to the mid-1990s.

Xiao Yang Zhang. *Shakespeare in China.* Newark: University of Delaware Press, 1996. An excellent survey of productions in China.

INDEX

About the Author
JAY L. HALIO is Professor of English at the University of Delaware.